New Green Homes

New Green Homes

Sergi Costa Duran

Ethel Baraona Pohl

Liliana Bollini

Introduction by:

Guillermo Hevia Hernández

COLLINS DESIGN

An Imprint of HarperCollinsPublishers

HarperCollins books may be purchased for educational, business, or sales promotional use.
For information, please write: Special Markets Department, HarperCollins*Publishers*,
10 East 53rd Street, New York, NY 10022.

First published in 2009 by:
Collins Design
An Imprint of HarperCollins*Publishers*
10 East 53rd Street
New York, NY 10022
Tel.: (212) 207-7000
Fax: (212) 207-7654
collinsdesign@harpercollins.com
www.harpercollins.com

Distributed throughout the world by:
HarperCollins*Publishers*
10 East 53rd Street
New York, NY 10022
Fax: (212) 207-7654

Editorial Coordinator:
Simone K. Schleifer

Assistant Editorial Coordinator:
Aitana Lleonart

Editor and texts:
Sergi Costa Duran, Ethel Baraona Pohl, Liliana Bollini

Art Director:
Mireia Casanovas Soley

Design and layout coordination:
Claudia Martínez Alonso

Layout:
Cristina Simó

ISBN: 978-0-06-192799-7
Library of Congress Control Number: 2009927945

Printed in Spain
First Printing, 2009

Index

Sustainability	7
Kingston House	8
Old Oaks Villa	14
Pentimento House	22
Mount Hotham House	30
Residence in Inverness	38
Villa Nuotta	46
House in Gerês	52
Rochedale House	60
X House	66
Gatica House	74
Skyline Residence	82
Ron-Ron House	92
Holman House	98
Cape Schanck House	106
House in Joanópolis	114
El Retorno Estate	120
House on Lake Rupanco	126
Big Dig House	132
Solar Umbrella	140
Greenfield Residence	148
Klein Bottle House	154
The Wave House	162
Johanna House	170
Panel House	176
Taroona 2	184
Sustainable Architecture Glossary	190
Bibliography	190
Directory	191

Sustainability

Global warming and the energy crisis are topics of great current significance and there is no doubt they are foremost in the minds of world leaders and authorities, and in public opinion in general. Sustainability is an issue that has come to the fore, although it is still not clear what this concept implies and whether it can be applied to all fields. What is important is awareness of these problems and how architecture can provide efficient response in a globalized world.

Can we claim that sustainable architecture exists? Is there enough awareness of the real urgency that exists for us to be able to respond to the demands of society?

I have my doubts. Discourse seems more important than convictions right now. Only real demand coming from society can bring about large-scale research and, consequently, drive us towards changing the current situation.

It is an undeniable fact that architects are presented with opportunities when it comes to creating our designs. We have the real and unavoidable responsibility to solve these problems in the measure of our technical and economic resources.

Nations face a very different reality. Some are equipped with technical and economic advantages, but also drawbacks, such as the lack of fossil fuel resources (oil and gas) and the high costs involved in satisfying increasing demands for development. However, this disadvantage can be turned to our advantage as it provides an OPPORTUNITY to use our imagination and find substitutes in passive energies, and other forms of energy that climate and nature have blessed us with.

Bioclimatic systems are alternatives that contribute to protecting the environment, saving energy, and improving our quality of life. There is no need to be overly complex. If we observe the ingenious solutions achieved by local architecture in different areas of the planet, we will have greater success and come that much closer to finding the appropriate solutions in our designs, which does not mean overlooking other solutions in this broad field of research.

The use of geothermal and wind energy systems to condition large industrial sites has produced good results in recent projects in a number of countries that are now at the international cutting edge (as is the case of Chile in South America). These projects have achieved remarkable energy efficiency levels compared with what had normally only been empirical exercises. Owing to their large size, industrial buildings permit interior environments to be controlled more effectively; they use more energy, and production costs accurately reflect this use.

Dwellings involve other complexities, and finding new solutions to them has become a matter of urgency. A large number of sustainable dwelling projects are being developed with sustainability parameters that range from the use of passive systems (solar energy and light, natural ventilation, etc.) to more complex technologies, such as computerized systems for solar shades on façades and the quest for greater energy self-sufficiency. Homes have different variables, such as size, location, and end use, influenced by different customs and cultures.

Development of dwellings must combine many qualities: they must adequately satisfy demand, provide solutions to the setting (urban and geographical environment), seek beauty and rational use of resources (natural, material and economic resources), respect cultures, and provide quality of life to people.

Architecture can offer imaginative responses to the challenges brought by global warming, and should be developed in a responsible manner by taking into account the problems facing the planet and attempting to produce the least impact on the environment and the immediate surroundings.

Guillermo Hevia Hernández is a Chilean architect who specialized in sustainable architecture at the Catholic University of Chile. He has pioneered solutions for large complexes and individual projects, for which he has received national and international recognition and prizes. Planta Cristalchile, one of his latest projects, received the distinction of *Highly Commended* at the World Architecture Festival held in Barcelona in 2008.

www.guillermohevia.cl / www.guillermohevia.blogspot.com

The symbols on each project's fact sheet refer to the following:

Energy   Water   Materials   Terrain   Climate

Kingston House

Room 11 Studio PTY LTD

Location **Kingston, Tasmania, Australia**
Surface area **2,570 sq ft**
Construction **2007**
© Jasmin Latona

Thermal inertia

Faucets with water-saving systems

Natural and locally sourced materials

Slightly sloping terrain

Temperate wet without a dry season

There are three central factors in the environmental strategy for this house: simplicity and lightness of construction, where predominant use is made of wood, natural or passive heating, and durability of the chosen materials.

The principal requirement for the project consisted of creating a retreat for its occupants who have a hectic urban lifestyle. The house had to have a strong relationship with the immediate and distant landscape. The response was a light building, resting on rather than supported by the rocky sloping terrain. It is a prism with several tree-filled courtyards. The trees provide shade and cool the air that flows inside the spatial volume.

Climate control revolves around natural mechanisms. To save on heating, the living area is set on a suspended concrete floor slab, which stores solar radiation and gives off heat during the night. The cooling strategy makes the best use of cross ventilation. The easterly and northerly breezes cross the house, as does with the cool air from the courtyards.

The choice of materials also takes into account environmental criteria. The wood on the horizontal walls comes from a plantation and factory in the local area. Another important material is concrete, chosen for its hard-wearing qualities and thermal inertia. The list is completed by glass and steel, highly recyclable materials.

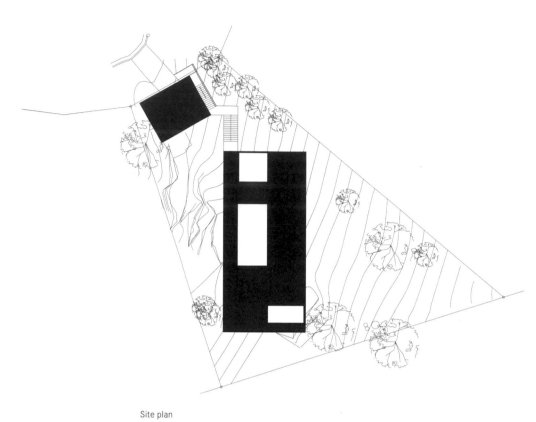

The dwelling is located on an abrupt and rocky site, covered in bushes and trees that, in the words of the architects, reach the interior through the courtyards so that they actively participate in the passive climate control strategy.

At times, it is only the change in materials that indicates where the house finishes and the natural setting begins. This boundary is established with two materials: locally sourced wood and stone from the actual site.

Only the glazed surfaces and the absence of a roof mark when one is inside or outside the house. Contact with the trees surrounding the plot, with only their crowns being seen through the elevation of the house, creates a strong connection between interior and exterior. Façades are sided with chipboard.

Site plan
Two structures were built on this steeply sloping, trapezium-shaped plot: a garage and a residence divided by a sequence of courtyard with intense vegetation. The house is a box-like structure that has been perforated to create raised walkways, decks and courtyards from which the landscape is perceived immediately and in the distance.

North elevation
The expanse of large floor-to-ceiling windows on the upper level are interrupted by a section of opaque wall, which gives weightlessness and light to the entire building. On the lower level, a louvered structure casts shade on the tree-filled courtyard.

South elevation
From this perspective, looking towards the highest part of the mountain, the house seems to lose the lower story, which is hidden by the slope. The composition is designed in three equal parts: one perforated, one transparent, and the other solid.

Site plan

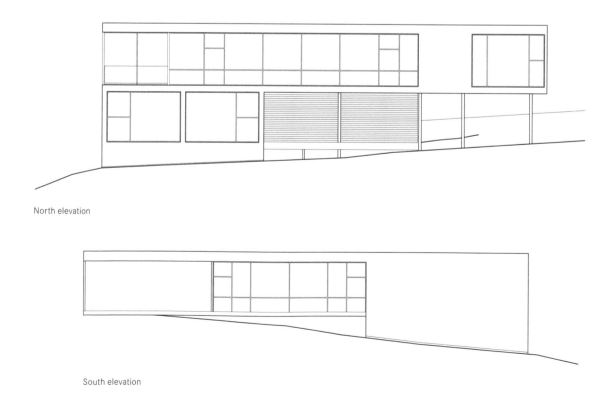

North elevation

South elevation

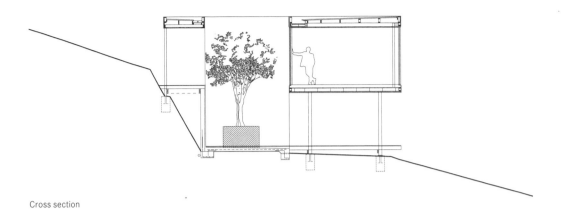

Cross section

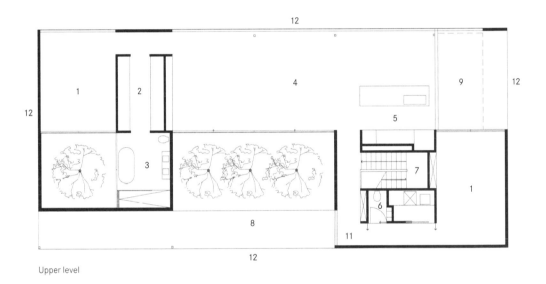

Upper level

The interior predominantly features extensive open spaces, designed with textureless materials in white, gray and black. Of note are the use of self-leveling cement in floors, enameled wood boards in furniture, plasterwork in ceilings, and artificial stone on countertops.

Maximum advantage has been taken of views. A large proportion of the external skin of the building is occupied by large glass surfaces, causing it to become almost transparent.

Cross section
The load-bearing frame is based on thick reinforced concrete slabs resting over beams and thin pillars made of metal. Foundations were laid as required and consist of separate bases at differing depths, depending on the slope.

Upper level
All of the common areas are found on the upper level: living area, kitchen/dining area, decks and external walkways. The master bedroom is on the level with the best views.

Lower level
Unlike most houses, this level does not contain the spaces mainly used during the day. Instead, it contains two bedrooms, the bathroom and the staircase. The remainder of the surface area is occupied by the courtyard and the open area between the pillars.

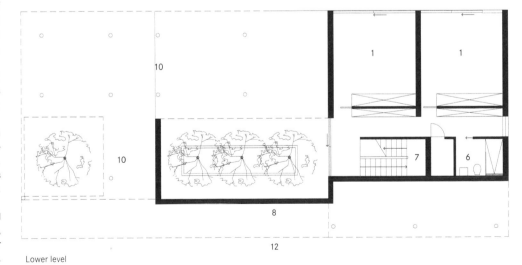

Lower level

1. Bedroom
2. Dressing room
3. Bathroom
4. Living/dining area
5. Kitchen/dining area
6. Guest bathroom
7. Stairs to bedrooms
8. Double height passageway
9. Deck
10. Courtyard
11. Entrance
12. Rocky slope

Old Oaks Villa

Ofis Arhitekti

Location **Ljubljana, Slovenia**
Surface area **8,610 sq ft**
Construction **2008**
© **Tomaž Gregorič**

Passive solar energy, maximum use of natural light, and automated louvers on the façade

Rainwater collection

Natural materials (oak and stone), plant-based varnishes

Slightly sloping terrain; existing trees preserved

Continental with average annual rainfall of 0.7 inch

This house is located in a new residential area of Ljubljana, made up of six residences with magnificent views of a wood of centenary oaks. As the terrain slopes down among these trees, in order to guarantee that most of the spaces of the house have access to the view, the rooms were laid out making use of the different levels of the site.

The dwelling was designed to take advantage of natural light and to maximize bioclimatic advantages. Weather conditions in Slovenia are extreme; temperatures can reach 35 °C in summer and -10 °C in winter, and there are heavy rains in spring and fall. The client's principal requirement was that the design should follow sustainable building guidelines, that it should deliver low energy consumption, and preservation of the natural resources of the place.

To achieve this, the spaces making up the house were laid out around a courtyard. This space is protected from the rain by a translucent roof that makes natural ventilation possible. As it is integrated in the surrounding woods, the courtyard stays at a pleasant temperature during the summer, while in winter, the trees having lost their leaves, the roof allows solar radiation to enter and heat the house, and other glassed spaces also permit sunlight to enter.

The façades were designed with the same idea. Louvers have been installed of wooden slats that pivot and vary their angle as required to provide solar protection and control the amount of light entering the dwelling. On the hottest days, the computer-controlled slats turn with the angle of solar incidence.

Cross sections (study). Utilization of the different levels of the dwelling for maximum adaptation to the terrain.

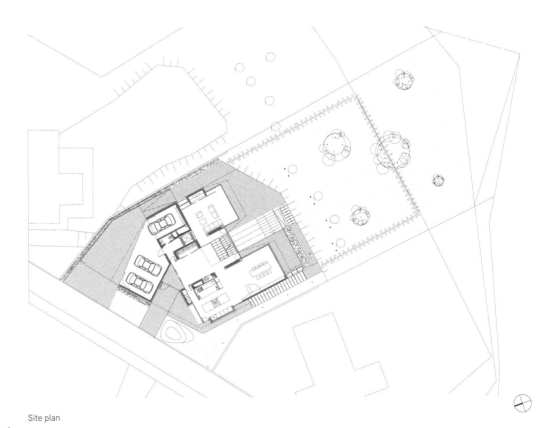

Site plan

The façade combines glass and wood.
The materials used are mostly natural and locally sourced: slate
and oak treated with ecological varnish.

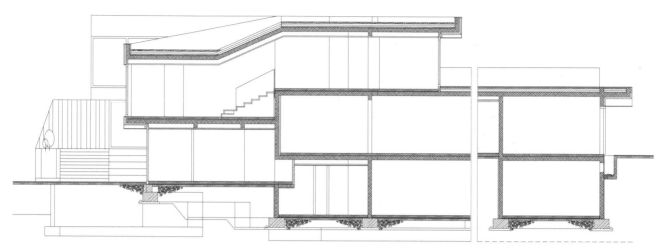

Longitudinal section

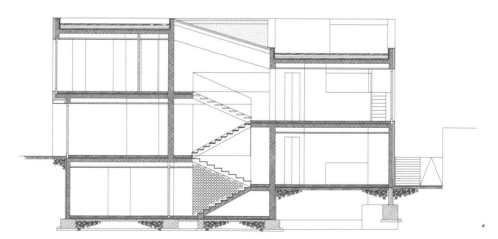

Cross section

Longitudinal section / Cross section
A layer of fine gravel was placed on the roof to absorb rainwater
and reuse it.

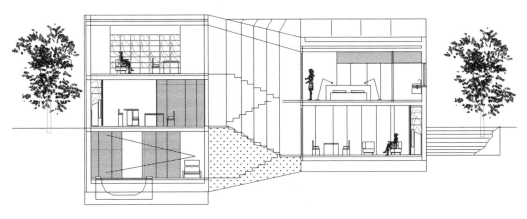

Cross section

All of the main spaces have views of the surroundings in an attempt by the architects to bring the forest closer to the interior of the dwelling.

The slats forming the brise-soleil filter the natural light in different ways, depending on the time of day or the corresponding season.

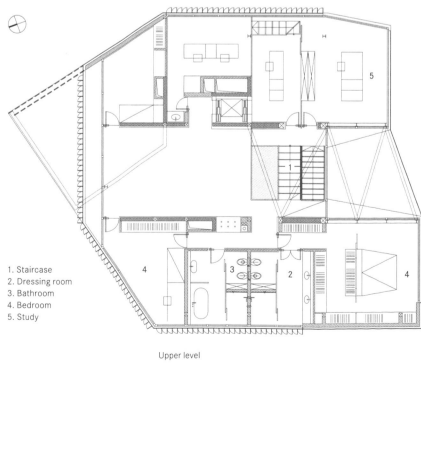

1. Staircase
2. Dressing room
3. Bathroom
4. Bedroom
5. Study

Upper level

When the louvers are closed, the façade gains uniformity and they are unnoticeable. When open, they provide a dynamic aspect.

The various perforations made in the roof of the reception area create different patterns in the light entering them. The use of fragmented panes creates reflections and allows good use of solar radiation.

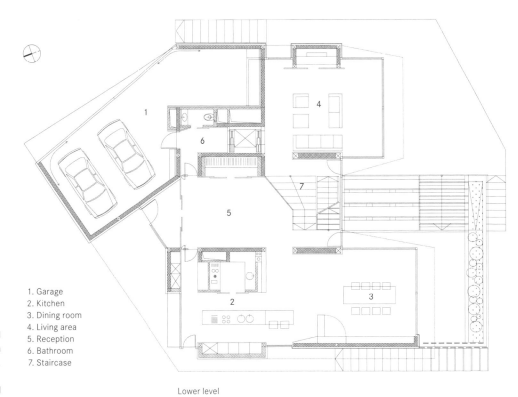

Upper level
Approximately 50% of the perimeter of the house is fitted with adjustable louvers.

Lower level
Common areas are found on the lowermost level of the house. The fact that these spaces are partially sunken into the ground guarantees optimal climate control.

1. Garage
2. Kitchen
3. Dining room
4. Living area
5. Reception
6. Bathroom
7. Staircase

Lower level

Pentimento House

José María Sáez Vaquero, David Patricio Barragán Andrade

Location **Quito, Ecuador**
Surface area **2,520 sq ft**
Construction **2006**
© **Raed Gindeya, José María Sáez**

Passive control systems for solar radiation

Prefabricated materials, dry assembly

Sloping terrain

Yearly average temperature of 12 °C

The architects had total freedom in the design of this house and the result is architecture that is harmonized with its setting. The dwelling was built as a single pre-cast concrete piece, providing a solution to the frame, walls, stairs and even garden front. From the outside, it is a neutral grid. Inside, each wall is different and is adapted to the needs of the different rooms.

The foundations make use of a concrete platform adapted to the heavily sloping terrain that incorporates the trees as part of the dwelling. The prefabricated system was raised over this platform. The pieces are reinforced with steel rods anchored in the platform. These rods and the joining elements create a tight structure of columns and lintels, which are suitable for the seismic conditions of the area.

The concrete is visible inside and out, and its hardness contrasts with the wood used in different spaces and the vegetation present throughout the house. The upper floor lookout allows air and light to enter and offers views of the distant mountains.

Passive energy-saving systems are present in the façade. Interstitial spaces remain open at some points and are closed at others with transparent acrylic and wooden strips. Temperature variations in the region where the dwelling is located are gentle; they oscillate between a maximum of 20 °C and a minimum of 9 °C, meaning the passive systems are sufficient to create comfortable interior climate conditions.

Sketch

The traditional granary was the principal source of inspiration for the dwelling. This is adapted to the terrain and landscape in such a way that the house is almost unnoticeable.

Site plan
The trees were preserved and even incorporated into the design.

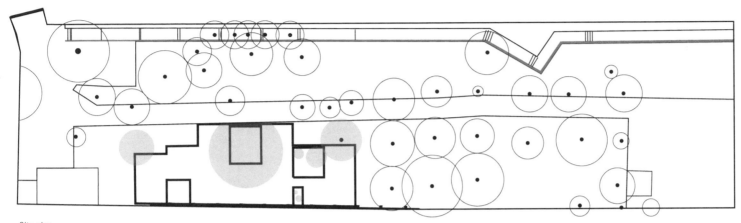

Site plan

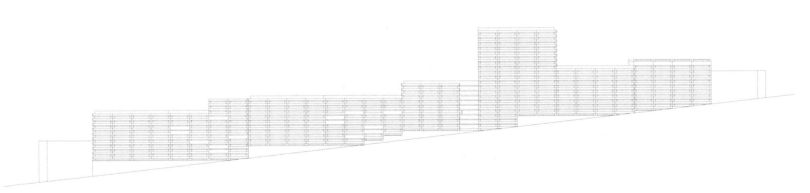

East elevation

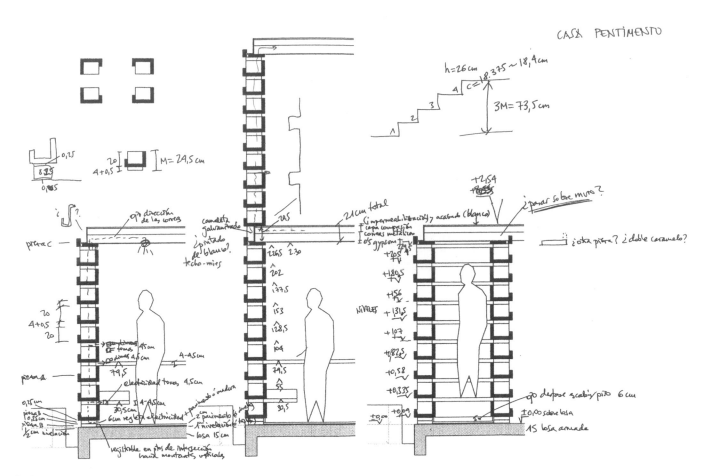

Draft design studying dimensions and layout of the elements making up the house.

During the day, light entering the house is filtered by the wall; at night, artificial light gradually illuminates the garden.

The contrast between extreme austerity and simplicity makes this project unique.

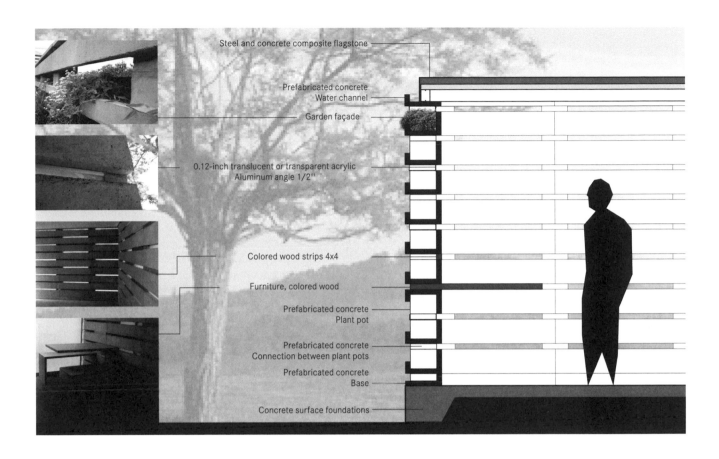

Steel and concrete composite flagstone

Prefabricated concrete
Water channel

Garden façade

0.12-inch translucent or transparent acrylic
Aluminum angle 1/2"

Colored wood strips 4x4

Furniture, colored wood

Prefabricated concrete
Plant pot

Prefabricated concrete
Connection between plant pots

Prefabricated concrete
Base

Concrete surface foundations

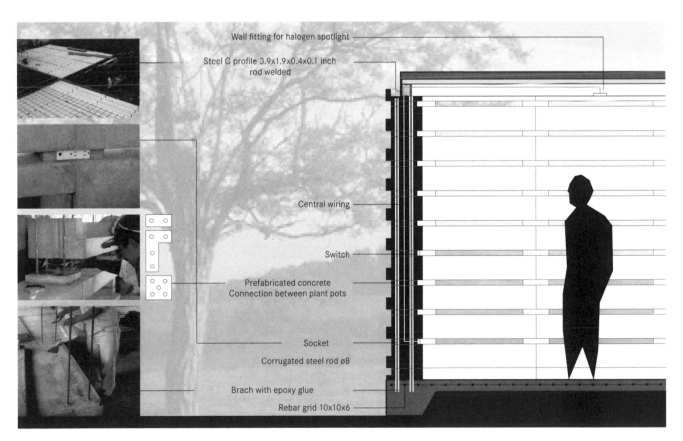

Wall fitting for halogen spotlight

Steel G profile 3.9x1.9x0.4x0.1 inch
rod welded

Central wiring

Switch

Prefabricated concrete
Connection between plant pots

Socket

Corrugated steel rod ø8

Brach with epoxy glue

Rebar grid 10x10x6

Explanatory sections: use and distribution of materials

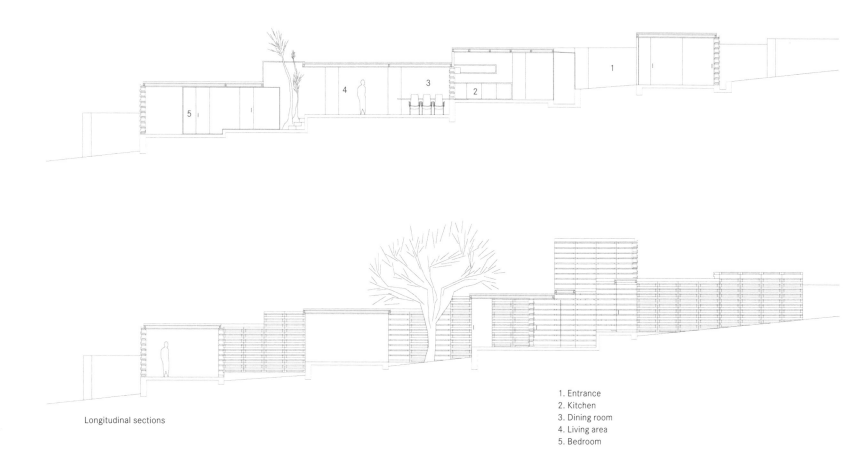

1. Entrance
2. Kitchen
3. Dining room
4. Living area
5. Bedroom

Longitudinal sections

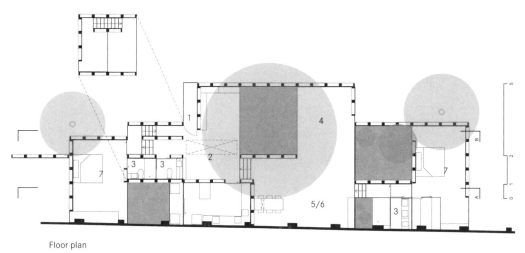

Floor plan

1. Entrance
2. Reception
3. Bathroom
4. Living area

5. Dining room
6. Kitchen
7. Bedroom

The same prefabricated element is utilized to give form to the walls and as a base for the furniture. The sense of play produced by terraces, courtyards and walls gives the house an interesting rhythm of solids and voids.

The courtyards are the climate control feature of greatest use in the design; they provide protection from the sun, plus ventilation and natural light.

Mount Hotham House

Giovanni D'Ambrosio

Location **Mount Hotham, Victoria, Australia**
Surface area **2,690 sq ft**
Construction **2007**
© **Giovanni D'Ambrosio**

Faucets with water-saving systems

Natural materials and materials with low environmental impact

Flat terrain

Temperate wet without a dry season

Built using steel, concrete, wood and local stone, the structure of this house is inspired by the architecture of Frank Lloyd Wright. The project had to fulfill a number of conditions. In addition to using local materials and typical features of the buildings in the area, it had to be comfortable in both summer and winter. Unlike most mountain houses, where windows are typically completely covered with blinds or curtains, this design makes great use of transparency. Large floor-to-ceiling windows allow the view to be enjoyed and merge the interior with the exterior.

The dwelling is divided into two levels. The lower level is given to common spaces, and from here it is possible to see the landscape framed by the windows and to access the deck. The upper floor contains two bedrooms, one of which is equipped with a spa.

There is a shelter in the car park. It is designed to be used during winter, when rain, snow, low temperatures and occasional storms predominate.

The project was developed with the requirement to produce the minimum impact possible on the natural environment. The roof is made of sheet steel and has significant thickness for the thermal insulation. Brown was chosen in its color scheme to favor insertion of the building into the landscape.

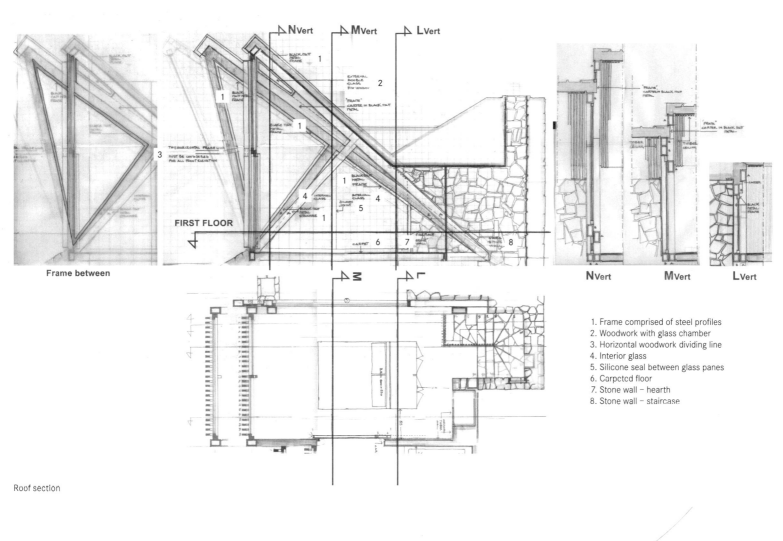

Frame between

FIRST FLOOR

Roof section

1. Frame comprised of steel profiles
2. Woodwork with glass chamber
3. Horizontal woodwork dividing line
4. Interior glass
5. Silicone seal between glass panes
6. Carpeted floor
7. Stone wall – hearth
8. Stone wall – staircase

Site plan

The only elements that stand out in this composition in relation to the landscape are the large black metal frames that follow the shape of the roof. The locally quarried stone in the walls are integrated into the setting. The broken form of the pitched roof and its steep incline, for the heavy winter snowfalls, give personality to the interior spaces.

Roof section
The roof is made from a frame of steel profiles and covered in steel panels.

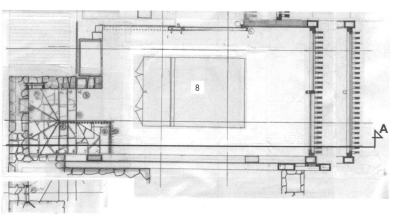

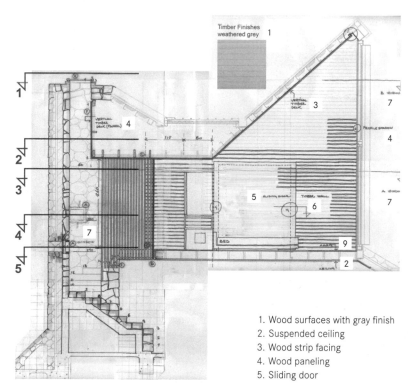

Timber Finishes
weathered grey

Staircase, dressing room, and bedroom plan.

1. Wood surfaces with gray finish
2. Suspended ceiling
3. Wood strip facing
4. Wood paneling
5. Sliding door

6. Wooden wall
7. Window
8. Bed
9. Carpeted floor

Staircase section

1. Garage
2. Reception
3. Bedroom
4. Bathroom
5. Dining room
6. Kitchen
7. Terrace
8. Living area
9. Bar/multimedia center
10. Void over living area
11. En-suite bathroom

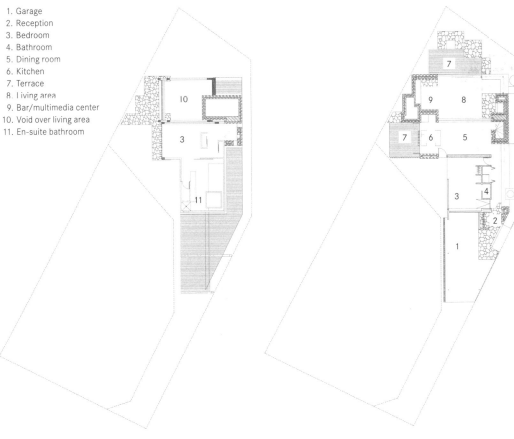

Upper level

Lower level

Upper level
On this level, the rooms are reduced in size and leave part of the roof visible. The staircase opens directly to the dressing room of the master bedroom, which has a very large bathroom fitted with a spa and a built-in day bed.

Lower level
Entry is through the garage. A reception area and hallway open to the double-height living area, the dining area, and the kitchen. The two main spaces have terraces.

Residence in Inverness

Studios Architecture

Location **Inverness, CA, USA**
Surface area **1,840 ft sq**
Construction **2004**
© **Tim Griffith, Michael O'Callahan**

Thermal inertia

Faucets with water-saving systems

Material sourced from the site

Terraced terrain

Mediterranean

This private residence is located on a steep slope only 407 ft away from Tomales Bay on the Pacific Ocean. The design of this house was inspired by the place and its historic rural buildings. The building is at once a wood cabin and a glass and steel tree house on stilts.

The floor plan, laid out lengthways, is made up of a series of interconnected volumes with different heights and materials. The intermediate spaces are adapted to the contours of the hillside. Each window and door offers a different sweeping view. The house is raised over a steel frame anchored to the hill, which allows good natural light to enter. The wooden roof and a projecting glass-enclosed space, containing the dining room, seem to float among the trees. The material used includes locally sourced Oregon pine.

Passive energy capture is enhanced by the window layout and the use of south-facing concrete walls, which store heat. This system is complemented by radiant floors.

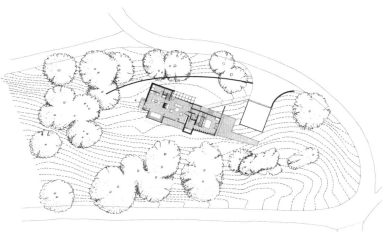

Site plan

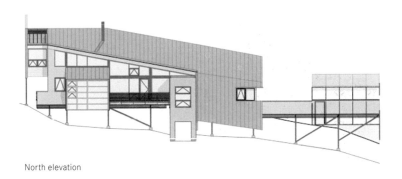

North elevation

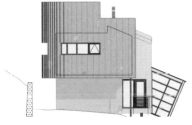

East elevation

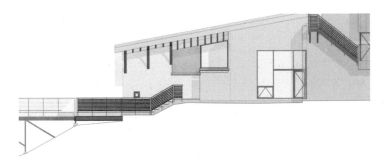

South elevation

The use of different materials on the façades — wood, exposed concrete, and zinc panels — together with the design of interconnected structures and full advantage taken of views are three aspects clearly expressed in the skin of the building.

Site plan
The intention to interfere as little as possible with the terrain and respect the slope and native plant species was a constant principle from the start of the project. This limitation did not hinder views of the landscape and passive solar energy capture, which was achieved through an ideal orientation.

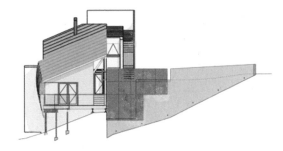

West elevation

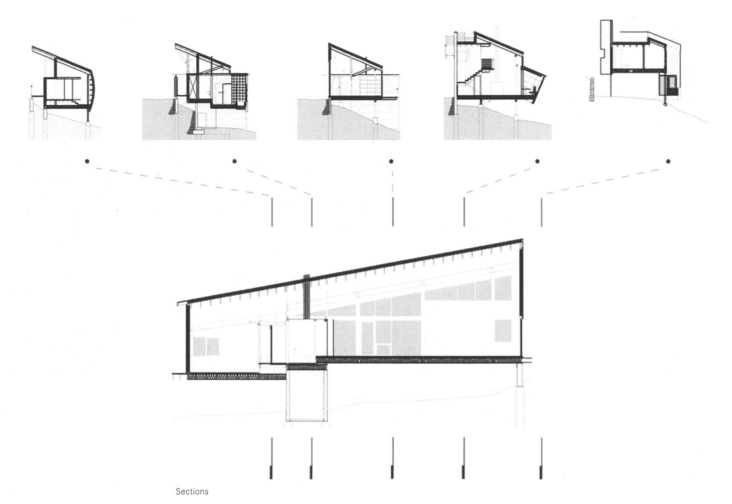

Sections

The exposed beam structure of the roof, the flooring, and the paneling on walls and closets are of treated wood which, combined with the steel frame, give a rustic and warm feel to the interior of the house.

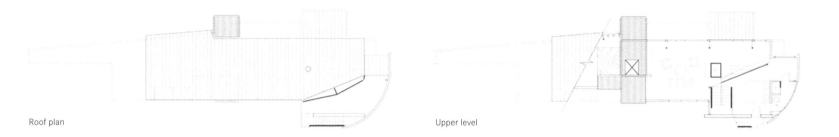

Roof plan

Upper level

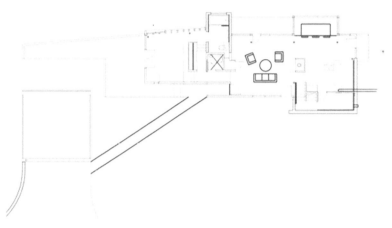

Lower level

The windows and enameled steel-framed glass doors enable the views of Tomales Bay to be enjoyed. The fireplace in the middle of the main living space serves to separate the kitchen-dining area from the lounge.

Lower level
The central axis runs through the house to finish at an observation deck on the east side. The driveway is separated from the main volume of the house, allowing the living-dining area to open to a patio that is sheltered from the street and with views of the bay.

Villa Nuotta

Tuomo Siitonen Architects

Location **Kerimäki, Finland**
Surface area **1,615 sq ft**
Construction **2007**
© **Rauno Träskelin, Mikko Auerniitty**

Passive solar energy

Certified sustainable locally sourced wood

Slightly sloping terrain

Temperate continental. Yearly average
temperature between 2 °C and 13 °C;
average annual rainfall of 2.8 inch

Villa Nuotta was built at the northern end of Herttuansaari Island, southeast of Kerimäki, between Lakes Puruvesi and Saimaa. The area is rocky and sterile, covered only by pines and marked by steeply sloping terrain. In the easternmost part, the hillsides fall abruptly to the coast and the setting is a mass of bushes and undergrowth. To the north, stones are covered with moss and lichens. Here a view can be enjoyed that is part of Natura 2000, a network of areas protected by the European Union.

The project was for the design of a vacation home, a residence used at certain times of the year by two adults and eventually by a number of friends. It can be used for work occasionally as it is equipped with all the necessary comforts.

To reduce the environmental impact to the minimum, the house was built entirely of wood certified by the Finnish Forest Certification Council, the Finnish system constituted by one of the largest timber suppliers in the world and guaranteeing sustainable forestry practices. The wood has two types of treatments: stained black with vegetable oil-based varnish, and varnished without pigments.

The terrain was not modified and the floor plan was adapted to it. A sunny patio serves as the entrance to the house and offers views of the lake. The split-level upper floor is comprised of superimposed planes. The sauna and guest room is on the lower, sunken level.

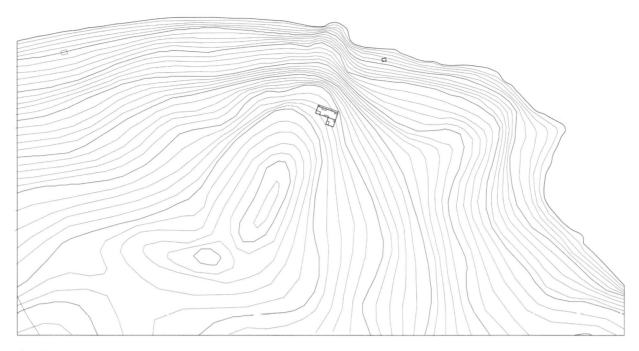

Site plan

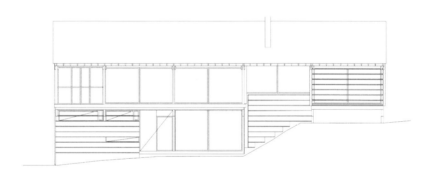

The house is on the top of a mountain. It is built of different kinds of wood and is perfectly inserted into the landscape.

Site plan
As seen from the contours, the dwelling is located nearly at the top of a mountain, on the edge of a cliff.

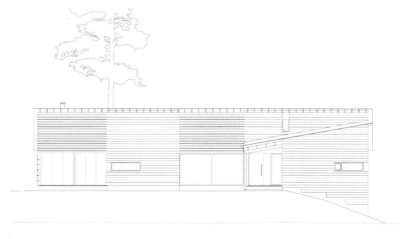

Elevations

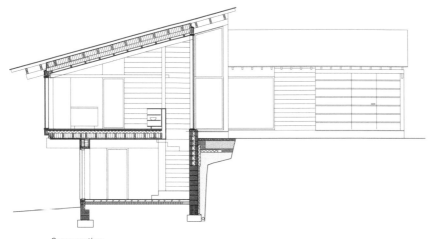

Cross section

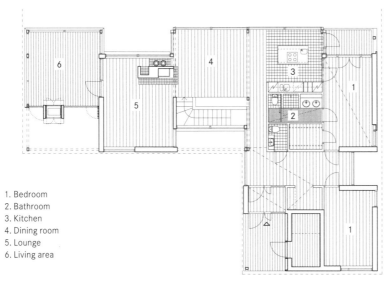

1. Bedroom
2. Bathroom
3. Kitchen
4. Dining room
5. Lounge
6. Living area

Upper level

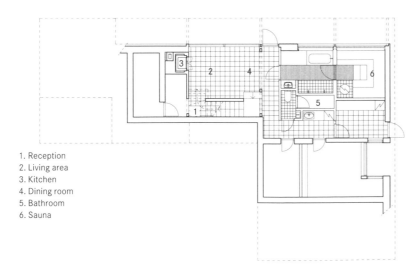

1. Reception
2. Living area
3. Kitchen
4. Dining room
5. Bathroom
6. Sauna

Lower level

Cross section
The house is fragmented over the site, so that it adapts to the terrain.

Upper level
Use is made of the spatial strategies to create areas receiving more sun and others receiving more shade.

The interior of the house is completely built of locally sourced wood finished in a clear varnish.

Natural materials are also used for the exterior — local sandstone is a perfect choice.

House in Gerês

Correia/Ragazzi Arquitectos

Location **Caniçada, Vieira do Minho, Portugal**
Surface area **1,615 sq ft**
Construction **2006**
© **Alberto Plácido, Juan Rodríguez**

Passive energy-saving systems, cross ventilation

Faucets with water-saving systems

Natural materials and materials with low environmental impact

Sloping terrain; existing trees preserved

Atlantic, cold and wet in the north

The project for this house consisted of the reconstruction of an old, dry stone building and the construction of a new structure on a site located in a protected natural area. The site had a number of particular conditions: a steep slope that made it necessary to anchor the building to the ground, and a grove of trees that had to be preserved.

The decision of how to intervene in a natural setting of these characteristics became the focus of the project. The clients soon showed their preferences for the exceptional views offered by the place, and the architects responded by creating spaces that, more than opening onto the landscape, seemed to be in it. The project consisted of a weekend house for a couple with a child and occasional visitors.

The location for the house was strongly limited by the existing building, which had to be respected, together with the trees. These conditioning factors, added to the intention of not carrying out any large-scale earthmoving or retaining structures, led to a volume (the prism container house) that was partly supported by the ground and partly cantilevered out. Both structures are of reinforced concrete and allow them to occupy a reduced area of the site. The volume has great visual permeability; rather than competing with the vegetation, it is integrated into it.

Site plan

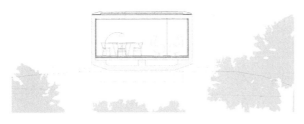

North elevation

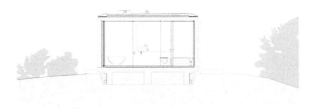

South elevation

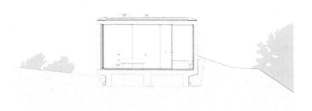

West elevation

The building nestles among the trees and overhangs from the hillside supported by a reinforced concrete pedestal. The site slopes so much that practically the only horizontal surface is the interior of the house.

The dining room cantilevered over the slope occupies approximately one third of the length of the house. To make this possible, the concrete structure took the shape of a bracket which, given its thickness, meant that had to be split level.

Site plan
Options for the house were limited, given that the space it occupied had to preserve the trees and the existing stone building, and because of the steeply sloping site.

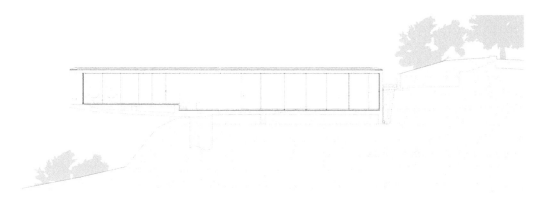

B-B section

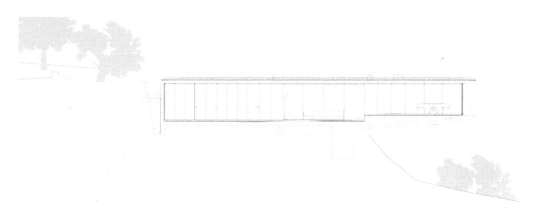

A-A section

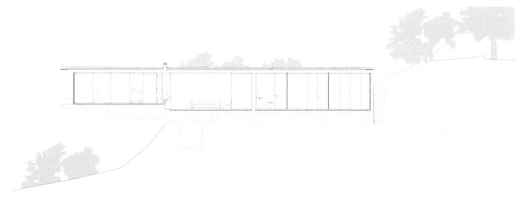

C-C section

The interiors of the new building and the restored older stone building are austere boxes where transparencies predominate, or facings of natural materials.

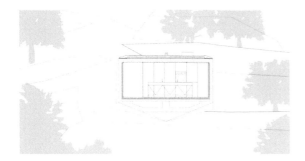

D-D section

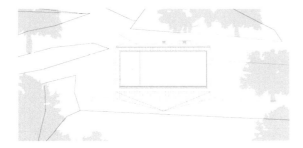

E-E section

I-I section

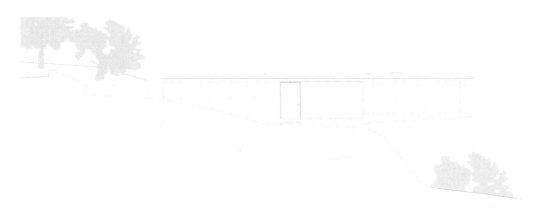

J-J section

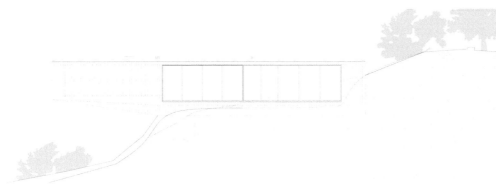

L-L section

Cross sections
If a longitudinal section is taken from rear to front, one can see the sequence of spaces: bedrooms, living area, kitchen and dining area.

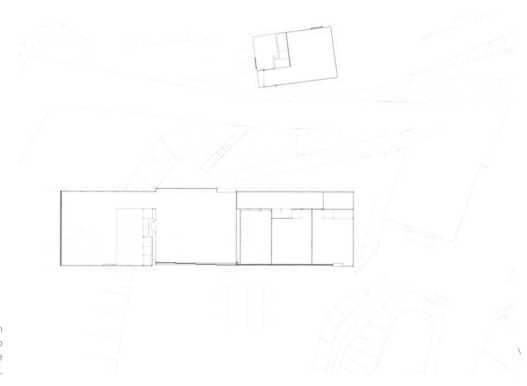

Not only the short side of the prism, open to the river, is in contact with the exterior. The long sides have been perforated to provide views of the scenery, and also to allow the volume to be see-through from the outside.

Floor plan

The smaller structure is a ruin with stone walls which was completely restored. In contrast, the larger volume containing the house is of new construction.

Floor plan

Rochedale House

Ray Kappe

Location **Brentwood, CA, USA**
Surface area **4,110 sq ft**
Construction **2007**
© **Living Homes, Gregg Segal, Valcucine**

Photovoltaic solar energy

Faucets with water-saving systems

Renewable, recyclable, non-toxic, and locally sourced materials

Slightly sloping terrain

Semi-desert with moderate temperatures and humidity

Living Homes is a company specializing in prefabricated houses using a steel frame that allows as many different spatial layouts as it does different combinations of materials. Rochedale House, designed by Ray Kappe, is an example of integration between manufacturer and architect. It shows how industrialization and the specifics of an architectural project can go hand in hand.

The residence is a joint development from Living Homes and *Wired Magazine*. Situated in Crestwood Hills, a neighborhood of modern homes in Los Angeles, the house is integrated into the setting by means of large glass surfaces and terraces that blur the lines between interior and exterior.

In addition to its novel construction system — prefabrication is taken to the level of workshop finishing, and the assembly of the modules can be done in only three days — the levels of environmental quality achieved by the houses built by Living Homes and designed by different architects are recognized by the most demanding categories of the prestigious Leadership in Energy and Environmental Design (LEED) certification system. Owing to measures such as the use of low environmental impact materials, quality of interior air, energy savings produced by the thermal insulation, solar protection, and renewable energy systems, Rochedale House achieves a reduction in energy use that is up to 36% of the standard and has been certified in the LEED Gold category.

The joint work of the manufacturer with material recycling associations will allow 76% of the material to be reused when the house reaches the end of its useful life and is dismantled instead of being indiscriminately demolished.

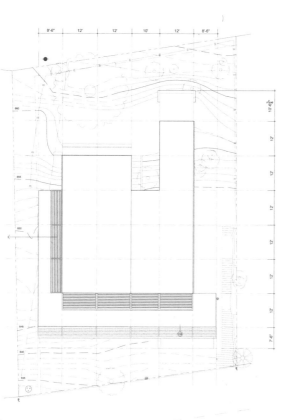

Site plan

Perspective

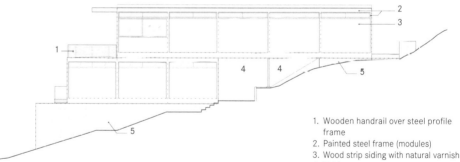

The prefabricated modules making up the volume of the house rest over poured reinforced concrete and cement blocks. Floor-to-ceiling windows provide a visual connection between interior and exterior.

1. Wooden handrail over steel profile frame
2. Painted steel frame (modules)
3. Wood strip siding with natural varnish
4. Void
5. Block wall, foundations

Site plan
Construction was adapted to the slope by means of sunken foundations and spaces. This platform with different levels allowed the installation of the modules to follow the stepped profile of the house.

Perspective
The dwelling is laid out over three levels adapted to the hillside: the lower level houses the garage and service systems; the middle level contains the bedrooms and their bathrooms; and the common areas made up of open-plan kitchen, dining area, living area, multi-purpose space and terrace are found on the upper level.

Cross section
The elevations show the layout of the house clearly. Of note are the prefabricated modules, which were delivered by truck, and assembled on site with a crane.

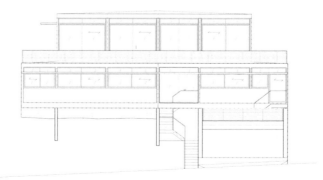

Cross section

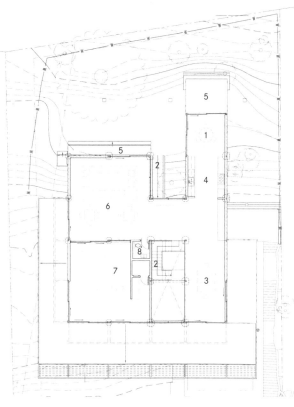

1. Breakfast room
2. Staircase
3. Dining area
4. Kitchen
5. Terrace
6. Living area
7. Multimedia room
8. Bathroom

Upper level

The interior design makes little use of decorative elements. This is coherent with the spatial composition and the simplicity of the construction: polished concrete floor, walls faced with plasterboard, and ceilings made of wood with natural varnish.

The structure of the prefabricated modules is visible in the living area. Here they are used to limit the spaces like screens. In the background is the access way to the terrace surrounding the upper level.

The ecological materials used in the dwelling are recycled steel and aluminum, glass partially made from recovered material, and certified sustainable wood treated with natural varnish.

Upper level
Highest level of the house containing the living and dining areas, kitchen, and terrace. All of the spaces have views of the street and nature, in addition to solar protection systems.

Lower level
This level is partially sunken and houses the garage, a plant room and the grid of slabs and interlocking beams of the foundations. Three staircases connect the upper levels.

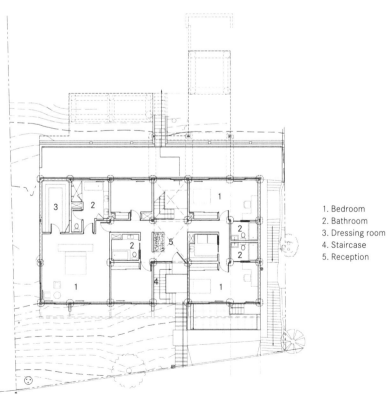

1. Bedroom
2. Bathroom
3. Dressing room
4. Staircase
5. Reception

Middle level

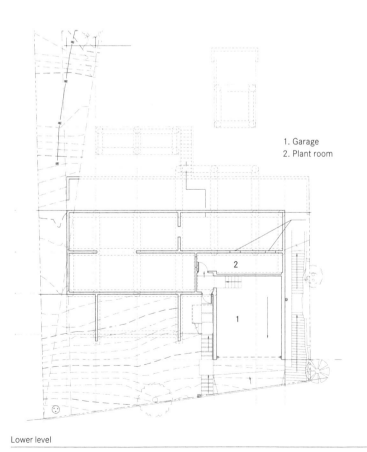

1. Garage
2. Plant room

Lower level

X House

Arquitectura X

Location **La Tola, Quito, Ecuador**
Surface area **4,090 sq ft**
Construction **2007**
© **Sebastián Crespo**

Evaporative cooling

Faucets with water-saving systems

Plant-based and recyclable materials

Flat terrain

Equatorial temperate and humid

The design of this dwelling was particularly special right from the start. The owners and architects did not have a definite site, meaning that the challenge was to design a house that would be equally suited to the Quito suburbs or the mountains to the east of the city.

For the Arquitectura X studio, this project involved an abstract design that synthesized a professional experience. "Inspired by the work of Donald Judd, an American artist who sought autonomy for the object, we proposed to locate an open box on any of the plots we would probably find, with spatial limits being the eastern or western mountain ranges. We then looked for a place we considered appropriate and found that the courtyard was the perfect creator of experiences in our professional history. In this way, the glass house works as a space with close limits set by the perimeter of the courtyard, and other distant limits established by the mountains. The incorporation of the courtyard into the design allowed us to adapt the house to the different sites it could be built on."

Common areas were separated form private spaces, and the central courtyard was turned into a focal point that ordered the service and transit areas. The side walls are made from multicellular polycarbonate, while the interior walls make use of plywood boards painted white.

The box built with plywood (common and marine) boards with an enameled Cor-Ten steel skin rests on foundations formed from reinforced concrete plinths and floor slab.

Exploded view

The study and library on the upper level are connected to the living area by a double height void. The floor is polished concrete painted white, while the ceiling and partition walls are made from galvanized steel profiles and plaster panels.

The glass box emerges from the inside face of the controlled rusting steel shell. Steps lead into the dwelling.

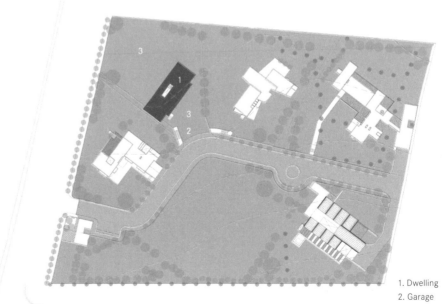

The side wall of the staircase is made from panels of laminated glass and 0.31-inch polycarbonate partitions with translucent and ice finishes. Door and window frames are of aluminum.

Steel columns support the white regular section beams framing the kitchen and the upper level study. The floor and ceiling are varnished plywood.

The different spaces are visually interconnected through double height voids. The upper level floor and the roof are concrete slabs supported by the steel frame. The interior is faced with 0.35-inch thick plywood.

Site plan
The house has an east-west orientation and is located on a large 15,930 sq ft site on the mountain range bordering the Tumbaco valley in Quito.

1. Dwelling
2. Garage
3. Terrace-garden

Site plan

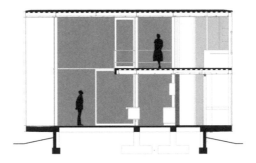

Cross section

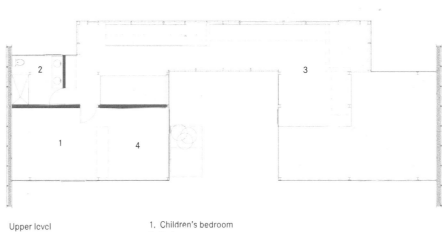

Upper level

1. Children's bedroom
2. Bathroom
3. Library/study
4. Games room (future bedroom)

The central patio was designed to contain a garden with plants and a pond. This natural feature cools the breezes penetrating the interior.

Cross section
The structural system is made from 6.3-inch HEB section steel columns resting on 7.9-inch IPN and regular section steel beams painted white.

Upper level
The children's bedroom, one bathroom, the study, and the library are located on this level. The transparency achieved by the walls and the double height voids create an important visual expanse throughout the entire level.

Lower level
The patio is the center of the house where two well-defined zones converge. The common area faces north. It consists of the living area, kitchen and entrance. On the opposite side is a bedroom and a second lounge area.

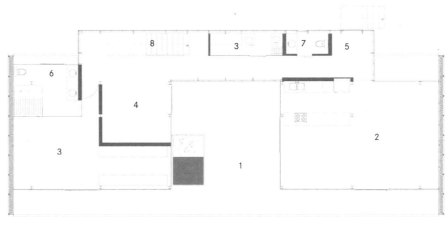

Lower level

1. Patio
2. Living/dining area/kitchen
3. Bedroom
4. Lounge
5. Entrance
6. Bathroom
7. Guest bathroom
8. Staircase

Gatica House

Felipe Assadi & Francisca Pulido

Location **Rancagua, Chile**
Surface area **5,920 sq ft**
Construction **2007**
© **Guy Wenborne**

Passive solar energy (orientation and inner patio)

Locally sourced materials (travertine marble)

Flat terrain; existing trees preserved

Warm temperate

This house is located in Rancagua, a city 54 miles south of Santiago. With temperatures ranging between a minimum of 5 °C in winter and a maximum of 30 °C in summer, the choice of materials and orientation was a basic element of the design.

A mixed program was requested of the architects: the owners needed a house that could be shared by two families. One was a married couple who would live in the house all year, and the other was a visiting family made up of three couples. The project was developed in two parts: The first was a linear design; it comprises the common areas and the master bedroom, rooms in use throughout the year.

The second part was not to be totally separate from the first, but should maintain a sense of individuality. A variable program was designed — a dwelling that was literally inserted into the main volume, but with use reserved for weekends.

Despite its relatively large dimensions, the house follows a single axis in its daily workings, but this is extended in accordance with the number of people living there on weekends and holidays. The volume design is a rectangular prism arranged lengthways. A group of elements were inserted that can be seen from both outside and inside the dwelling. The black volume is independent from the others, both in form and structure.

Predominant use was made of glass and metal. Inside, the floors are of wood with natural varnish, while the exterior walls are clad in black slate. Outdoor ground cover is locally produced gravel. The decking around the swimming pool is made from certified wood.

A dramatic combination of volumes was used in the design of this house. One of these overhangs the other, held up by slim metal pillars that call to mind Le Corbusier's Villa Savoye.

The semi-interior patio allows natural light to enter the common areas of the house; at the same time, it also creates shade during the hottest hours of the day owing to its orientation. Use of natural materials like black slate is one of the strong points of the project.

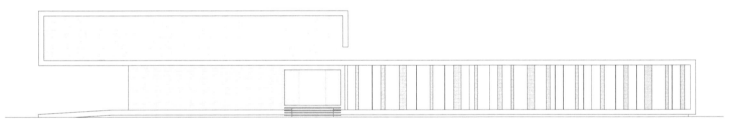

North elevation

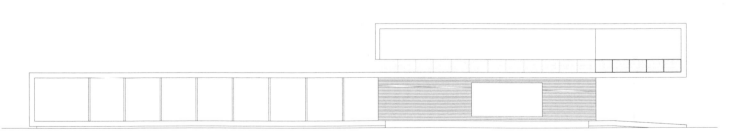

South elevation

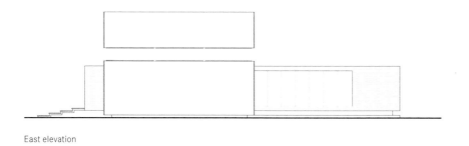

East elevation

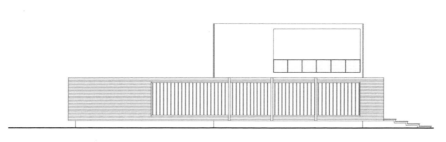

West elevation

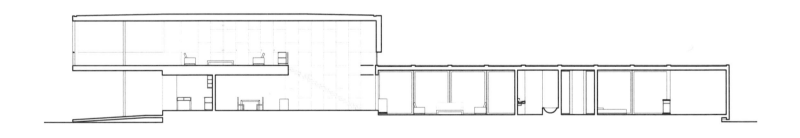

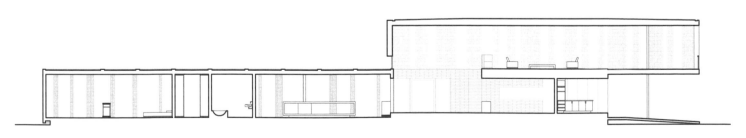

Longitudinal sections

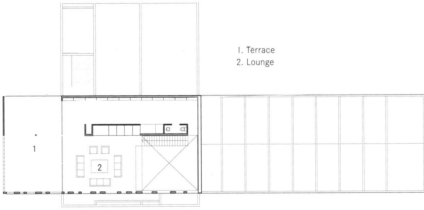

1. Terrace
2. Lounge

Upper level

Longitudinal sections
Fluidity is enhanced in the design of the spaces, which are united
by a double height in the stairwell.

Lower level

1. Bedroom
2. Bathroom
3. Kitchen
4. Dining room
5. Living area
6. Dressing room

Skyline Residence

Belzberg Architects

Location **Los Angeles, CA, USA**
Surface area **5,800 sq ft**
Construction **2007**
© **Benny Chan/Fotoworks, Belzberg Architects**

Passive solar energy, cross ventilation

Faucets with water-saving systems

Material sourced from the site

Terraced terrain

Temperate Mediterranean and dry all year around

The Skyline Residence is located in the Hollywood Hills. It is open to the northwest where it overlooks downtown Los Angeles, Laurel Canyon, and the San Fernando Valley. The main residence and guesthouse are situated on a narrow linear plot that abuts a steep hillside on two sides.

The premise of the design was protection from the harsh direct sunlight and the layout of spaces to make full use of views. In fact, the positioning of walls revolves around this. Each room has magnificent views of the surroundings through large floor-to-ceiling glass walls.

The difficulty of the terrain and the dense granite below the surface permitted only minimum excavation for the foundations, which was also among the priorities of the project. The removed granite was decomposed and reused to level drain pipes under the concrete slab. It was also used as a drainage field under the infinity pool and on the viewing deck over the garage.

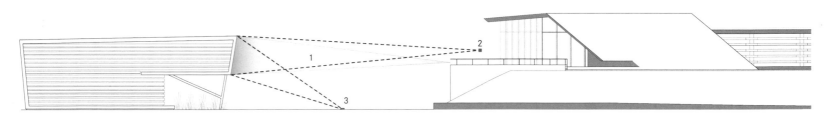

Cross section. Study of heights and distances in relation to an outer wall.

1. Projection
2. Viewing deck
3. Auto court

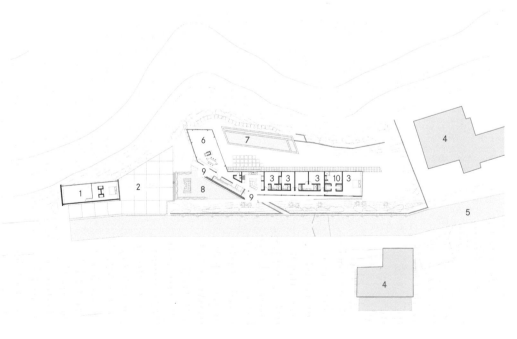

Site plan

The Skyline Residence is barely visible from afar. Its placement in the middle of a natural setting is very subtle. The main house and the guesthouse share the same social space but are two physically differentiated volumes.

The choice of locally sourced material was a priority to avoid the environmental impact of transport. The choice of vegetation was for low water use (xerogardening).

1. Guest house
2. Garage
3. Bedroom
4. Neighboring houses
5. Driveway
6. Living area
7. Pool
8. Terrace
9. Entrances
10. Kitchen/dining area

The orientation of the building allows each room to have a full glass wall. The opposite side faces southwest and has spaces protected from solar radiation by overlapping slats.

Large eaves extend over the sides of the main house and cast shade over the glazed surfaces.

Because the living area is laid out with numerous openings, it takes on the characteristics of an exterior space, not only physically but visually. The sparing use of furniture adds to the effect.

Thermal buffer placed between the inner skin of the bedrooms and the exterior create a ventilated area that is protected from the sun.

Solar incidence diagram
The blue lines indicate glazed walls on the north and east. The façade is opaque on the sides that are most exposed to solar radiation.

Solar incidence diagram

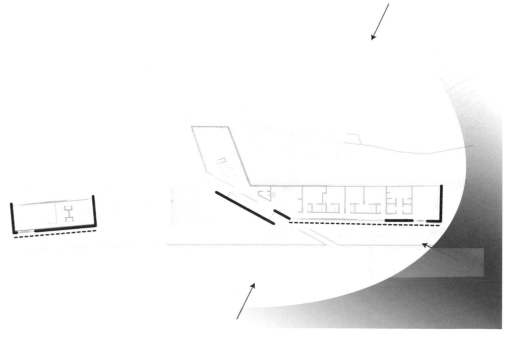

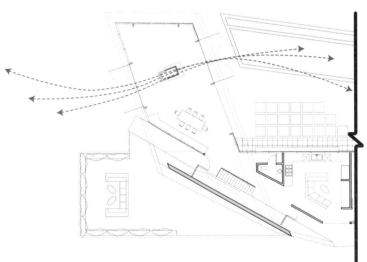
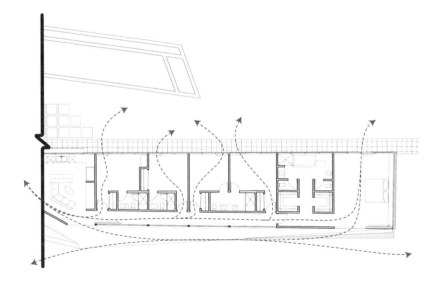

Diagram of the house's natural ventilation.

The wind coming from the valleys enters the house from both sides and produces a sensation of being outdoors. This is accentuated by the placement of large glass doors in the living area.

The pool is visually connected to the living area through large floor-to-ceiling windows. Magnificent views over Los Angeles can be appreciated from inside.

Diagram of the house's natural ventilation Good use is made of prevailing winds in the area to ensure adequate circulation in all rooms, avoiding the need for air conditioning and reducing total energy use in the house.

Ron-Ron House

Víctor Cañas, Andrés Cañas

Location **Golfo de Papagayo, Costa Rica**
Surface area **4,520 sq ft**
Construction **2007**
© **Jordi Miralles**

Thermal solar energy, cross ventilation

Certified sustainable locally sourced wood

Sloping terrain

Tropical with wet and dry seasons

A house bearing the name of a tree native to Costa Rica reminds us of how far a natural space, regardless of how small it is, can be the motive for the design of a space. Nature is perceived from the house in two ways: close, if one looks at the specimen of ron-ron or *Astronium graveolens*, and far, if the view takes in the sea sprinkled with islets.

As the site is bordered by a cliff facing the Pacific Ocean on one side, and a street on the other, the design opted to open the house to the sea so that nearly all of the rooms face in that direction and are buffered from the noise of passing vehicles. The house has two levels: the bedrooms are on the upper level and the common areas are on the lower floor. At one end, separated from the rest of the house by a wooden bridge over a swimming pool, is the guest room. The garage, also designed as a free-standing volume, completes the set.

The living area, dining room and kitchen occupy most of the lower level and form a single space, although they are differentiated by small changes in floor level or walls of medium height. These spaces are directly connected to the pool and the large terrace where the ron-ron tree stands. Upstairs, a series of internal wood and glass bridges overlooking the lower floor lead to the bedrooms. This complex spatial layout, which lies on steeply sloping terrain, is borne by a series of pillars, interlocking beams, and reinforced concrete foundations anchored to the rock.

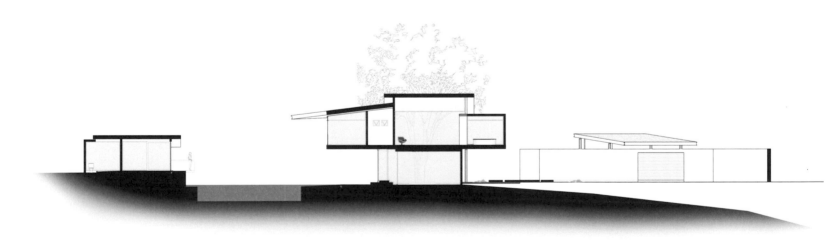

Longitudinal section

Longitudinal section
The excavation into the hillside and the cliff are not visible in the area parallel to the sea. The simplicity of the layout is seen in the sequence of guest bedroom, swimming pool, house, garden, and garage.

Cross section
The very narrow site offered practically no horizontal surface area on which to place the house. To achieve this, the hillside had to be excavated and it was necessary to build cantilevered structures held up by supports anchored in the rock.

Cross section
The very pronounced slope of the site and the intense rainfall during the wet season meant the house had to be separated from the hillside. In this way most of the rainwater flows into the sea.

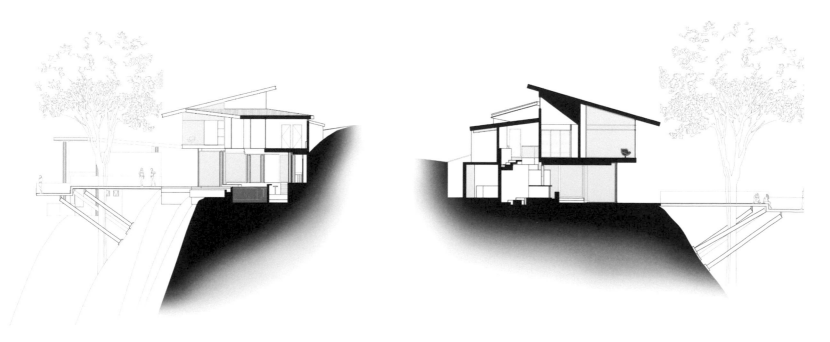

Cross section

Cross section

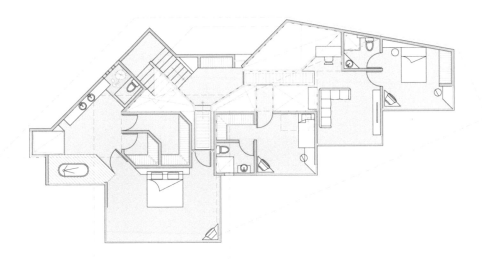

Upper level

The long layout and zigzag façade accentuate the dimensions of the house. The use of swirled or rustic reinforced concrete on ceilings, walls, and floors contrasts with the transparency of the glass.

The relation between interior and exterior is often defined by great expanses of wall-to-wall and floor-to-ceiling glass, permitting the spaces on the lower level to merge with the terrace and the bedrooms to enjoy views of the Gulf.

The difficult relationship between the large expanses of glass and the tropical climate were resolved with roof eaves, which protect from the intense solar radiation.

Upper level
A series of bridges on the lower level connect the bedrooms. This design is repeated on the upper level. Each of the rooms faces the Golfo de Papagayo with their backs to the path.

Lower level
The house nestles into a narrow strip between a path and a cliff facing the sea. The volume of the dwelling makes the most of the available space by winding along the former and rising over the latter.

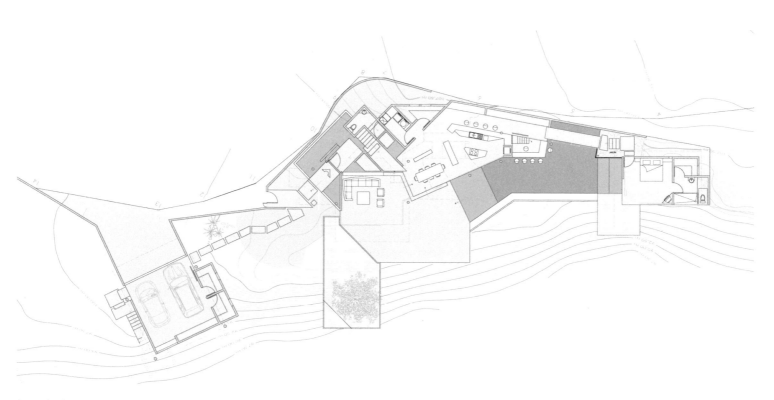

Lower level

Holman House

Durbach Block Architects

Location **Dover Heights, Sydney, Australia**
Surface area **3,498 sq ft**
Construction **2005**
© **Brett Boardman, Anthony Browell, Reiner Blunck**

Passive solar energy

Natural materials (wood and stone)

Sloping terrain

Temperate oceanic

Dover Heights is a residential suburb located only 5.6 miles away from central Sydney. Holman House is perched on the edge of a 230-ft cliff. The architectural project takes full advantage of the site. Its design is open to the sea, and the sea breeze provides cross ventilation. The interior spaces arc and fold in response to the rocky landscape. These features, combined with an austere choice of materials, give the design a restrained feel.

Despite its location in a built-up area, Holman House stands out from other dwellings in its particular way of adapting to the terrain, with a design that makes the most of all of the environmental advantages of the setting. It is anchored to the cliff as if it were another rocky outcrop; the rooms are adapted to the variety of curves to achieve optimal orientation of windows for light and ventilation; and the use of concrete as the base material means that the house works like a thermally insulated box, particularly at night when the temperature drops.

Living areas cantilever out to provide excellent views of the coast. The walls of the lower floor are of rough stone, like an extension of the cliff. These walls, worked with local techniques, follow the edge of the cliff to form a series of terraced gardens. The swimming pool is located on a lower level in a space created by the curves.

Interior finishing is in natural materials. The lower level is practically carved into the rock, which increases the thermal inertia of the walls in contact with the earth.

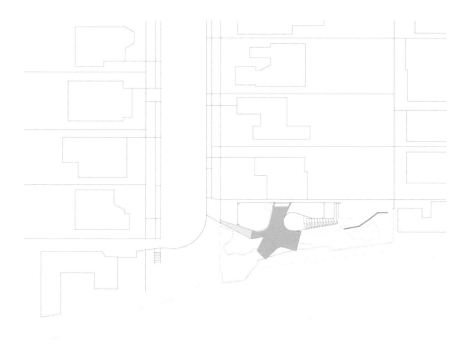

Site plan

The distinguishing feature of Holman House is the cantilevered section that projects beyond the cliff, towards the sea.

The living area has a glass façade. On the other side, where sunlight is more direct, the size of the windows is reduced and these play a secondary role.

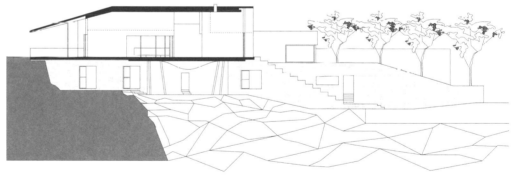

East elevation

Instead of retreating back from the cliff, Holman House is the only dwelling in the area to be built over it and with its shapes in dialogue with it.

East elevation
The lower level, where the bedrooms are located, is in direct contact with the cliff rock.

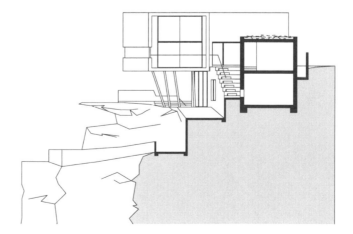

Cross section

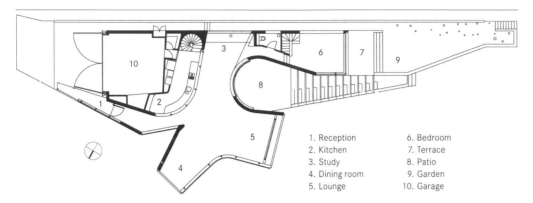

1. Reception   6. Bedroom
2. Kitchen   7. Terrace
3. Study   8. Patio
4. Dining room 9. Garden
5. Lounge   10. Garage

Upper level

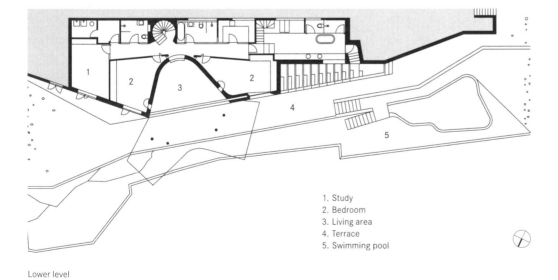

1. Study
2. Bedroom
3. Living area
4. Terrace
5. Swimming pool

Lower level

The walls in direct contact with the rock have greater thermal inertia, which is used to heat the interior on cold nights.

The living and dining areas are located inside the cantilevered volume.

The totally open interiors have an austere design that leaves the windows and the ocean views as protagonists. The furniture and floors contain local and certified wood. The glass was formed at high temperatures to achieve the degree of curvature required by the design.

Cape Schanck House

Jackson Clements Burrows Architects

Location **Cape Schanck, Victoria, Australia**
Surface area **4,306 sq ft**
Construction **2006**
© **John Gollings**

Passive solar energy, home automation

Rainwater collection for domestic use, use of groundwater for garden watering

Material sourced from the site

Slightly sloping terrain

Temperate without a dry season

Cape Schanck is a place characterized by heath and dunes with areas of low vegetation. The original landscape, previously inhabited by aborigines, was modified by the first European farmers settling in the region. The area presently has a high risk of fire owing to strong solar radiation and drought. In fact, on their first visit to the site, the architects encountered the remnants of burnt-out logs, which became their source of inspiration. The house recreates a hollowed log.

The design responds to the needs of a retired couple who receive regular visits from children and grandchildren. The dwelling is laid out over two levels: the lower level or base of the building, where guest accommodation and a central plant controlling the service systems are located; and the upper or primary level containing the remaining areas.

Both levels feature interior wood paneling treated with oils and stained black. The cedar windows have also been treated with natural products to produce a black grain and create a weathered effect.

The house faces northwest and there are sweeping views from all of the rooms. To control excessive solar radiation in summer, the windows are protected by louver blinds that descend automatically once the sun passes through the north axis of the house. Other *eco-efficient* considerations are the automated systems that reduce energy use from climate control needs. Here, they control temperature regulation and starting up. Bore water is used for the garden and swimming pool, while rainwater is collected and treated for domestic use.

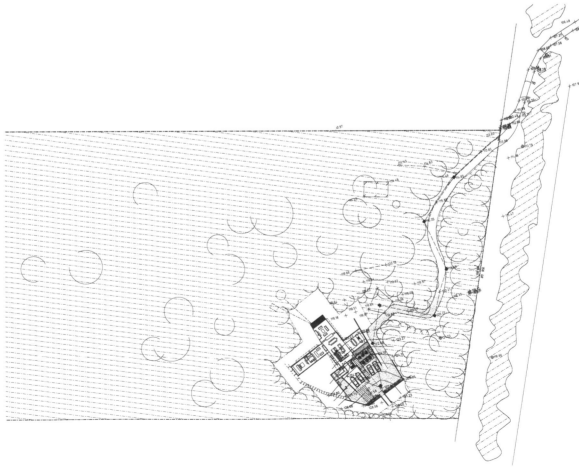

Site plan

The house has the height of a single level and does not stand out from the landscape. The shell is clad in black weathered wood that has been treated with oils to resist harsh climatic conditions.

The design of the house is based on the shape of a tree. The wooden wall becomes a visual screen and purposefully hides the terrace and swimming pool.

Site plan
The project makes use of a large sloping site, allowing the house to take the shape of a hollow log facing northwest.

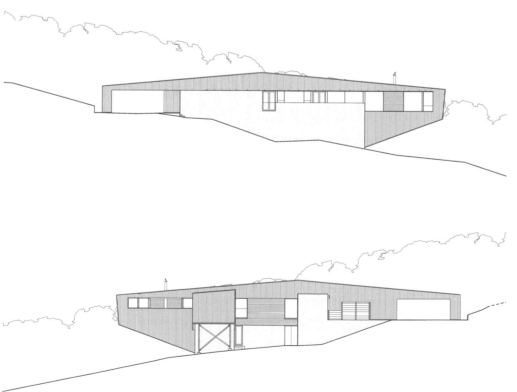

The prolongation of the shell over the terrace serves to protect
it from the sun. The outdoor walkways and roof are of treated
wood, while the outer walls are clad in black metal panels.

Elevations
The house follows the sloping terrain and is reached through its
highest point. Owing to the slope, the main rooms are several
meters above the ground, arranged as balconies over the valley.

Longitudinal section
Independent foundations allow concrete slabs and metal floor
structures to be laid out as required. The frame of the inner and
outer walls is raised over these, and the walls in turn support the
latticed members of the roof.

Elevations

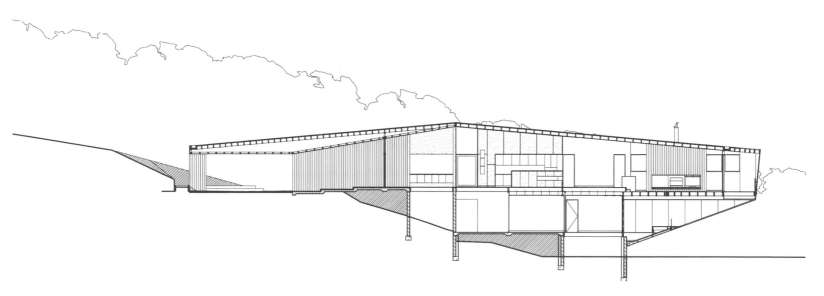

Longitudinal section

Exterior and interior are in continuous dialogue through extensive floor to ceiling windows.

Upper level
The kitchen, dining room, living area, garage, and laundry are located on this level. Branching off from this are the study and bedroom suite.

Lower level
The lower floor contains guest rooms and functional spaces where, for example, the pool equipment is located.

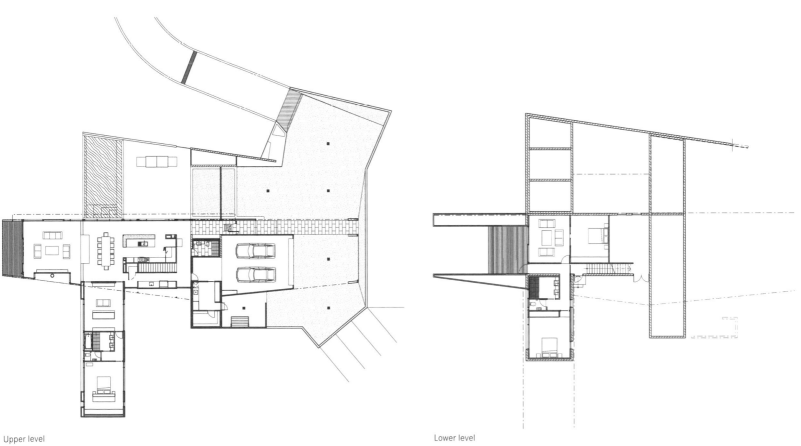

Upper level

Lower level

House in Joanópolis

Una Arquitetos

Location **Joanópolis, São Paulo, Brazil**
Surface area **4,670 sq ft**
Construction **2008**
© **Bebete Viégas**

Thermal inertia

Rainwater collection

Locally sourced materials, traditional-style use of stone

Slightly sloping terrain

Subtropical, yearly average temperature of 19°C

Joanópolis House is located in the border region between São Paulo and Minas Gerais, more specifically at the end of the foot of the Mantiqueira Mountains, at an altitude of 3,280 ft. The house is part of a residential development on the shore of Lake Piracaia. Houses in this type of residential development are typically designed to occupy most of the plot, leaving little space between one house and another. The starting idea for the design of this house was precisely the opposite: adapt the structure to the sloping terrain and create a house with ease of transit, far away from the other dwellings. Earthmoving was used on the site and the excavated earth was used in areas where filling was needed.

Embankment walls were built with stone found on site and using local techniques. Three patios maintain a direct relation with the interior spaces of the house. A white tower is clearly visible from the street. It holds the service infrastructure (kitchen, flues, water tank, and heaters). This structure rises from a horizontal plane measuring 26 x 131 ft, which is a roof garden. This guarantees effective thermal inertia in a place with large differences between day and night temperatures.

The long frame is made from reinforced concrete, modulated in spans of 13 ft. The walls and finishes were built in keeping with the cost-saving premise of the design. The inherent qualities of the materials were also respected and unnecessary finishes were avoided.

The stone walls were built using traditional techniques, and all of the bathrooms are located in the same area, which means energy savings in the functioning of the dwelling. The structure standing out from the roof is the water storage tank.

The house is inserted into the landscape as the result of a suitable choice of materials and design of the spaces. Both the front and rear have glazed façades that enhance cross ventilation.

The swimming pool is located at one end of the site, in a completely open area with sea views, in contrast to the courtyards located at the other end.

Site plan
To minimize impact to the site, the house follows the contours and its orientation is ideal to take advantage of sea views. Both green roof and gravel-lined roof increase the thermal mass of the building and act as natural climate control agents. Native vegetation is planted in gardens: peroba-rosa, jequitibá, embaúba, aroeira, tarumã, ipês, grumixaba, caroba, acacia and jacaranda. A series of fruit trees were planted in outdoor areas closest to the house: jabuticaba, Surinam cherry, orange, lemon, pomegranate and acerola.

Front
There is constant contrast between solid and transparent surfaces. The stone and concrete base form a pedestal for the rest of the house, as if it were a sculpture.

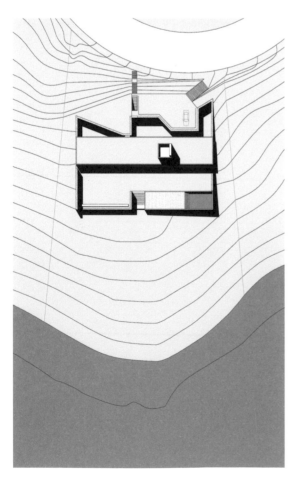

Site plan

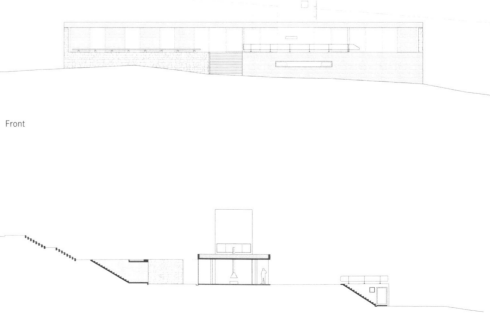

Front

Cross section

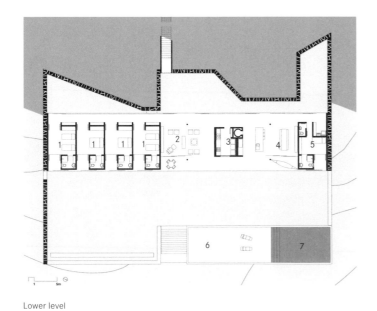

Lower level

1. Bedroom
2. Living area
3. Kitchen
4. Dining room
5. Bathroom area
6. Terrace
7. Swimming pool

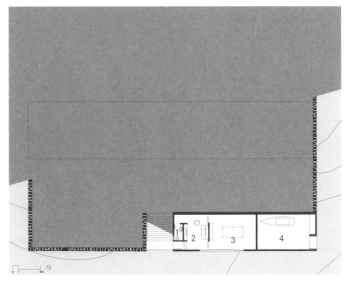

Extension

1. Bathroom
2. Living area
3. Game room
4. Boat storage

The glass surface was withdrawn 6.6 ft from the space limiting the façade, allowing the projecting roof to form a porch for protection from the sun.

In the south-facing rear of the building, the porch is no longer necessary. The stone walls shield the house from strong winds.

Gravel paving in the courtyards also act as thermal storage, as they absorb heat during the day and release it in the interior at night.

El Retorno Estate

G Ateliers

Location **Antioquia, Colombia**
Surface area **2,850 sq ft**
Construction **2008**
© **Gustavo Valencia**

Passive solar energy, cross ventilation

Rainwater collection

Natural (oak and stone)

Sloping terrain

Cold and wet

These two dwellings form part of the first stage of a project for eco-shelters in Guatapé, a municipality in Antioquia Department, located 49 miles from Medellín and with good potential for the development of ecological tourism. Their placing in this setting conditioned the design, consisting of a series of shelters immersed in the surrounding forest and offering the opportunity for escape from the hectic pace of the city to relax and contemplate the scenery.

The design has its base and reasoning in the value of the area's beauty: architecture should be fully adapted to its environment. Consequently, several types of shelter were proposed, all centered on the same concept — preserving nature — but with structures that varied depending on the terrain. These shelters are perfectly adapted to the topography, as if they emerged from the terrain. In order to minimize the environmental impact, the roof structures were conceived as extensions of the mountain. The floor plans respond strictly to making good use of solar energy, achieving considerable energy savings.

The use of traditional elements of Colombian architecture, such as perimeter corridors, creates a dialogue between architecture, man, and landscape. The spatial layout is optimal and takes full advantage of the available habitable space of each shelter. It also encourages cross ventilation, particularly during the summer months.

These two shelters make up the first stage of the project. A second phase is projected to include six more shelters, a restaurant, and a chapel. All of the buildings — including the shelters — will be connected via a series of paths.

The structure is perfectly adapted to the terrain. The stairs and passageways surround the dwelling, which is traditional in Colombian architecture. Views of the landscape can be appreciated from the perimeter passageway.

The upper part is a green roof which, in addition to integrating the dwelling into the setting, insulates it from solar radiation and regulates the temperature inside the house. The planter boxes along the perimeter of the roof are part of a water collection system that is enough to satisfy needs for water in the house.

The main materials utilized for the exterior are glass, reinforced concrete, and aluminum, the latter two rendered in stucco and painted black.

Site plan
Complete plan of the project, where shelters 1 and 2 can be seen in addition to those to be built in the future. Emphasis is given to the way the structures adapt to the contours of the terrain.

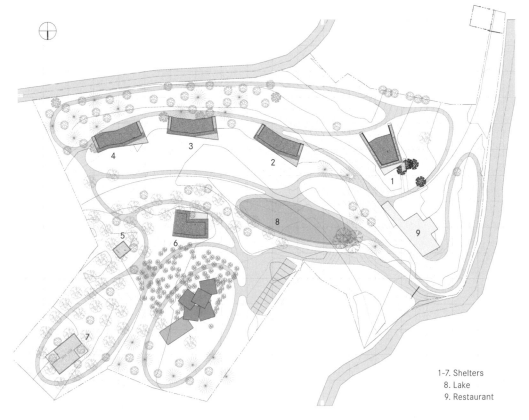

Site plan

1-7. Shelters
8. Lake
9. Restaurant

Predominant use is made of oak facings on ceilings and walls, with slate floors.

A-A section
A design adapted to the environment was achieved in a simple way.

Roof level
There are three skylights in the roof through which sunlight is filtered into the interior of the dwelling.

Lower level
North-facing spaces make the best use of sunlight and views of the forest, while the south side is partially sunken to provide natural climate control inside.

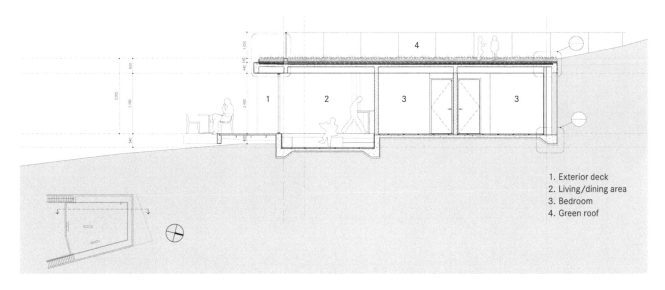

1. Exterior deck
2. Living/dining area
3. Bedroom
4. Green roof

A-A section

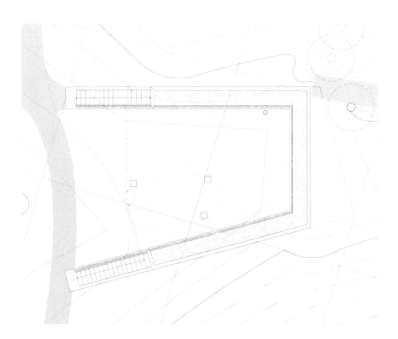

Roof level

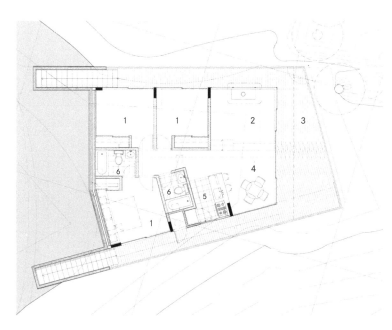

Lower level

1. Bedroom   4. Dining room
2. Living area   5. Kitchen
3. Terrace   6. Bathroom

House on Lake Rupanco

Beals Arquitectos

Location **Lago Rupanco, Región de Los Lagos, Chile**
Surface area **3,010 sq ft**
Construction **2006**
© **Alejandro Beals**

Passive solar energy, maximum use of natural light, cross ventilation

Natural materials (pine, mañío and ulmu wood)

Sloping terrain

Temperate wet

This house is located on the shores of Lake Rupanco in southern Chile. The region is generally characterized by a temperate wet climate, with temperature varying between 9 °C and 18 °C. The plot measures 525 x 98 ft with a 118 ft slope and has views over the south of the lake. The orientation of the house takes full advantage of these views. The principal façade is glassed to create a visual connection with the lake. The rear of the building is lost in a forest of Chilean myrtles and native shrubs.

Certain similarities to the Reutter House by Matthias Klotz can be noticed in this dwelling. The entrance is reached over a wooden footbridge bridge placed on the upper level at the end of a path running through the trees until it reaches the house. Dense vegetation on the sides isolates the house from surrounding dwellings.

The interior gives priority to the master bedroom and the living area, the two spaces with the best views. There is double height in the living area, which provides greater entry of light and natural ventilation. On the east face, a garden separating the two bathrooms divides the prism in two parts. This creates a play of volumes that allows natural light into both rooms.

The design borrows on shapes and textures of traditional building styles in the area: barns, stables, and dairies (Hacienda Rupanco dairy farm is located on the southwestern shore). The frame of the house is in pine, and the façades are in impregnated pine. The interior walls are clad in untreated mañió and ulmu wood.

The exterior walls have been treated with a waterproofing technique common to rural buildings in southern Chile to protect it from the persistent rainfall in the area.

The typical barn structure found in the area served as inspiration for the shape of this house. The frame was worked almost completely from wood; only a few metal elements were used to help provide greater stability.

Owing to the use of local wood, and despite the box-like shapes, the building is integrated into its setting. The south façade opens to the lake.

Isometric view
The frame of the house is made from pine.

South elevation
This facade is almost completely glazed as it offers views of the lake.

North elevation
The lower level is practically detached from the exterior, while the upper level has balconies to allow views of the Chilean myrtle forest.

West elevation
The house is adapted to the terrain through its design on different levels. A wooden bridge at the entrance overcomes the difference in height at this part of the site.

East elevation
Most of the windows are arranged around a semi-enclosed patio, because it has the ideal orientation to take advantage of morning light.

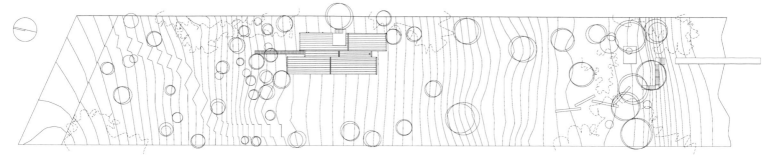

Site plan

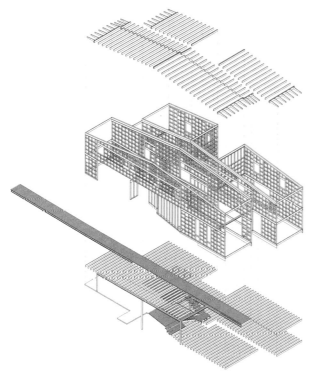

Isometric view

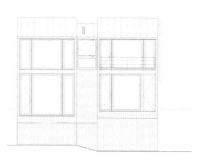

South elevation

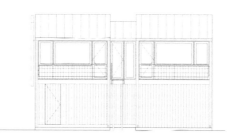

North elevation

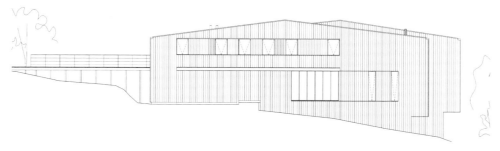

West elevation

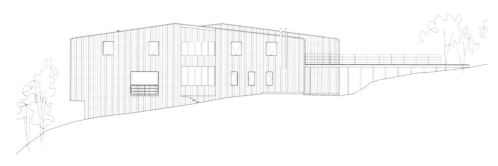

East elevation

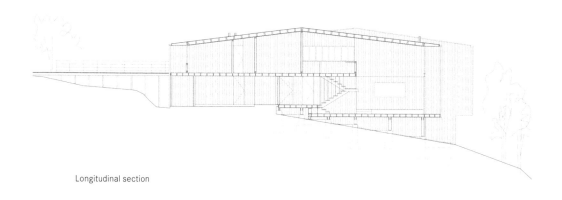

Longitudinal section

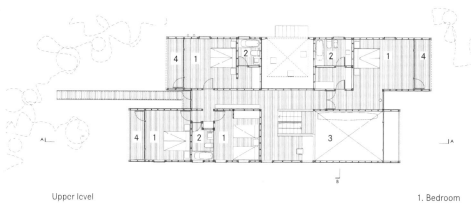

Upper level

1. Bedroom
2. Bathroom
3. Double height
4. Balcony

The interior open-plan spaces are also faced with wood, which gives it warmth and counteracts the damp location. The translucent design of the staircase gives a feeling of more interior space.

Longitudinal section
The foundations of the different parts of the house had to be made with piers that vary in height depending on the variations in the terrain.

Upper level
This floor has four bedrooms that are interconnected by a central passageway.

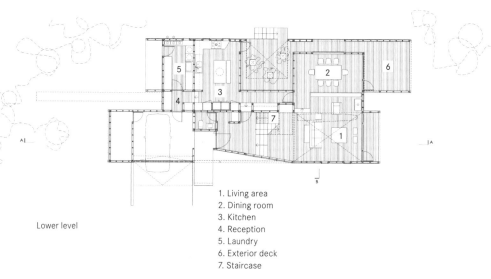

Lower level

1. Living area
2. Dining room
3. Kitchen
4. Reception
5. Laundry
6. Exterior deck
7. Staircase

Big Dig House

SSD – Architecture + Urbanism

Location **Lexington, MA, USA**
Surface area **2,420 sq ft**
Construction **2006**
© **SSD – Architecture + Urbanism**

Passive solar energy

Rainwater collection

Material recovered from other building sites

Flat terrain; existing trees preserved

Humid continental

The Big Dig is the largest and most complex infrastructure project carried out in the United States. It is also considered to be the most technologically challenging highway plan in the world. The project includes two bridges over the Charles River (with fourteen lanes), a steel tunnel under Boston Harbor, the demolition of an older highway and the creation of over one hundred hectares of parkland and open spaces.

In this context, Big Dig House was built as a prototype dwelling using recycled material and made use of material salvaged from the Big Dig site. Steel and concrete were used for the frame. The dry assembly system meant that the house was built in three days instead of the three weeks that would have been needed if traditional systems had been used. This amounted to time and energy savings of 35% of the total cost.

The project shows that materials can be adapted to passive cooling and heating systems. The double height of the living room is heated with solar radiation, and radiant flooring has been laid in all of the rooms. A water storage system has been created in the garden where water accumulates in a cistern and is used to water the patio areas.

Although this project is only a family residence, its design encourages the reuse of waste material from infrastructure works in schools and multi-dwelling projects. On an urban scale, the environmental and cost-savings benefits in labor and materials would multiply to the degree that it would be possible to implement more projects like this one.

1

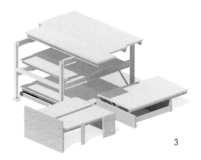

2

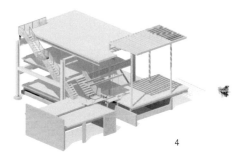

3

4

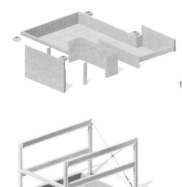

5

The façade is characterized by its apparent simplicity of shape. There is widespread use of wood and glass, and the concrete plinth contrasts with the metal frame.

The frame of the house is made of metal beams and columns, which form a structure that is independent of the interior walls.

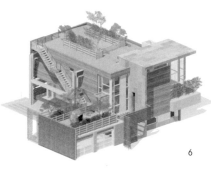

6

1. Laying foundations
2. Frame
3. Slab floors
4. Staircase
5. Roof garden
6. Cladding

Assembly sequence

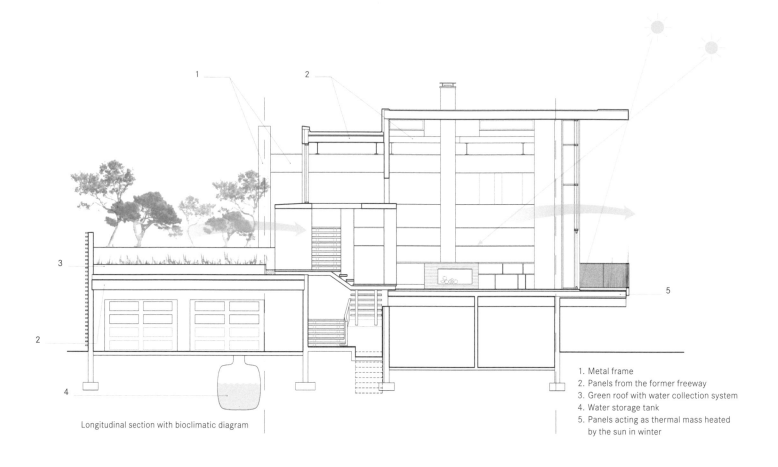

Longitudinal section with bioclimatic diagram

1. Metal frame
2. Panels from the former freeway
3. Green roof with water collection system
4. Water storage tank
5. Panels acting as thermal mass heated by the sun in winter

An exterior staircase connects the garage with the roof garden. It is supported by an imposing metal frame.

Inside, the double height in the stairwell acts as a climate control feature by means of the thermal chimney effect.

The slabs supporting the roof are pieces of precast concrete that were previously part of a demolished freeway ramp. A close-up look can be seen from the mezzanine level of the large industrial pipes used for the flue. The staircase is made of metal treads and struts, which also serve as handrails. The large salvaged metal beams can also be seen in the interior.

To make maximum use of natural light, large windows have been used in common areas.

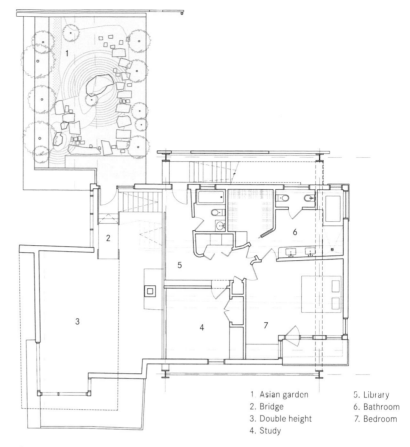

1. Asian garden   5. Library
2. Bridge   6. Bathroom
3. Double height   7. Bedroom
4. Study

Upper level

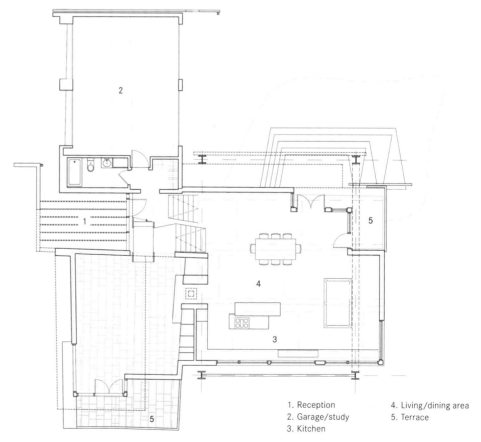

1. Reception   4. Living/dining area
2. Garage/study   5. Terrace
3. Kitchen

Lower level

The kitchen area has both floor-to-ceiling windows and a skylight, which ensure the ventilation of the room. There is a pool table next to this area.

Solar Umbrella

Pugh & Scarpa

Location **Venice, CA, USA**
Surface area **1,290 sq ft new
construction + 646 sq ft remodeling**
Construction **2006**
© **Marvin Rand**

Photovoltaic solar energy, maximum use of natural light

Rainwater collection

Natural, recyclable and eco-efficient materials

Flat terrain

Arid and dry

This dwelling was inspired by the Umbrella House, designed by Paul Rudolph in 1953, with a reinterpretation of the roof. The aim was to offer maximum protection to the interior of the house from harsh solar radiation. Consequently, the architects analyzed every detail of the opportunities offered by the site and made use of as many sustainable parameters as they could incorporate into the design to create a highly energy-efficient and comfortable dwelling.

The design of active and passive solar protection elements is based around the broad roof of photovoltaic panels that protect the house and give a name to the project. The 89 photovoltaic panels cover 95% of energy needs. A heating system connected to this network feeds radiant flooring laid in a remodeled part of the house. At the same time, the roof shades a large part of the dwelling and protects it from the heat. Three photovoltaic panels are used exclusively for heating water for domestic use, and a fourth panel heats the water in the swimming pool.

80% of the water collected on the roof is stored. The plants used in outdoor landscaping are native species requiring little watering. Outdoor spaces have been paved sparingly and greater use has been made of gravel, which allows rainwater infiltration.

During construction, another element taken into account was waste management. About 85% of the water produced was recycled. Material left over from refurbishment to the original house was used in the construction of the extension. Most of the materials used were natural: stone, locally sourced wood, and mineral-tinted stucco, among others.

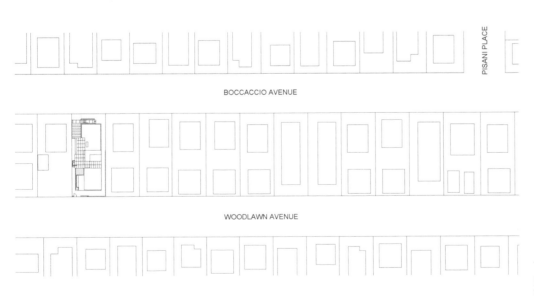

PISANI PLACE

BOCCACCIO AVENUE

WOODLAWN AVENUE

Site plan

Through sliding glass doors, the living area opens to a patio of approximately 194 sq ft. The front of the house faces Woodlawn Avenue.

Photovoltaic solar panels cover the entire roof of the house and even other parts of the façade.

Site plan
The dwelling was built in a neighborhood with similar plot sizes and terrain.

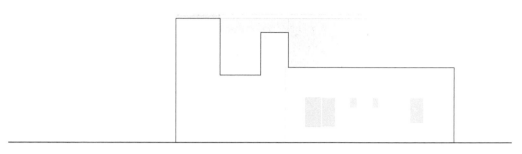

North elevation

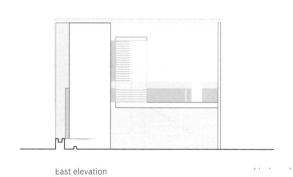

East elevation

South elevation

South elevation
This is a good example of how photovoltaic solar panels are
integrated into the façade as a solar protection element.

West elevation

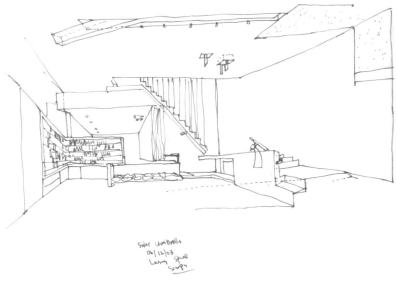

Drawing 1

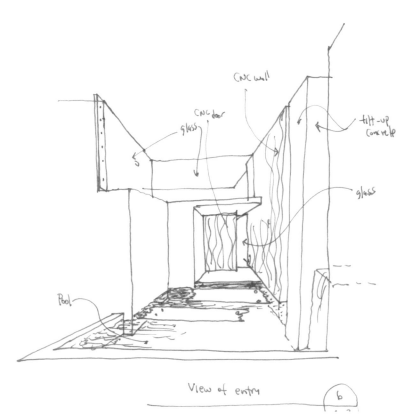

View of entry

Drawing 2

The front entrance is varnished with plant-based oils. Open interior spaces favor cross ventilation. The metal staircase is a dividing element between the new construction and the renovated part. Its weightless design allows light entering from a skylight to be appreciated.

Drawing 1
The interior of the house was built as projected in initial drafts, showing coherence in the project.

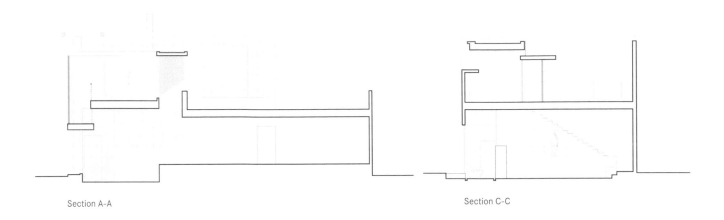

Section A-A

Section C-C

Roof plan

1. Photovoltaic panels
2. Roof
3. Skylight
4. Lower level roof
5. Patio

Upper level

1. Bedroom
2. Bathroom
3. Bath
4. Closet

5. Patio
6. Roof
7. Skylight

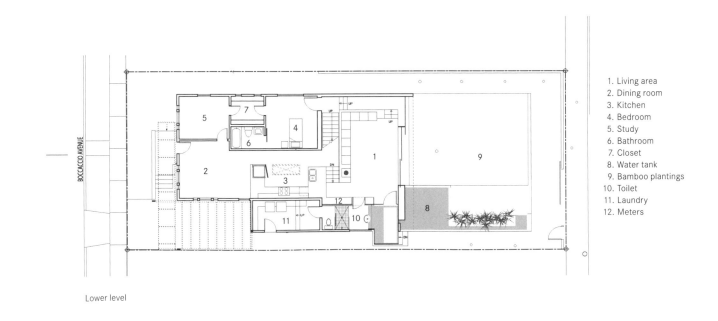

BOCCACCIO AVENUE

Lower level

1. Living area
2. Dining room
3. Kitchen
4. Bedroom
5. Study
6. Bathroom
7. Closet
8. Water tank
9. Bamboo plantings
10. Toilet
11. Laundry
12. Meters

The furniture in the master bedroom is made from boards of formaldehyde-free, high-density fiber.

The floor in the kitchen and living area is of Oriented Strand Board, a material made from wood chips.

Section A-A / Section C-C
Interior spaces are extensive and laid out to provide unhindered cross ventilation and natural light.

Greenfield Residence

Minarc Aarchitects

Location **Los Angeles, CA, USA**
Surface area **3,767 sq ft**
Construction **2007**
© **Erla Dögg Ingjaldsdóttir, Ralph Seeberger, Bragi Joseffson**

Maximum use of natural light, radiant floor heating

Faucets with water-saving systems

Recyclable, recycled and organic materials; plant-based varnishes

Flat terrain

Mediterranean with wet winters and dry summers

The Greenfield Residence is a house designed by Icelandic architects Minarc, who have lived and worked in the United States for over ten years. Among the outstanding features of this house is the appropriate use of materials. A pleasant atmosphere has been created in all of the spaces through a range of innovative materials. The stairs are covered in blue rubber, traditionally used for coating the handles of hammers. This open-plan and minimalist design is meant to reflect the cold waters of Icelandic waterfalls. The interior walls are clad in certified wood treated with plant-based varnishes. Corian, a recyclable material with low volatile organic compound (VOC) content is used in the kitchen, an open space that takes maximum advantage of natural light. Kitchen cabinets and chairs are made from fibers sourced from recycled tires.

The layout of interior spaces is vital to enable maximum utilization of the built surface area. The lower floor was designed to open up common areas. The living room and kitchen form a single space with cross ventilation that also reaches the dining area. This is located on the outside to take advantage of the climate of Santa Monica, where temperatures vary between 20 °C and 37 °C, depending on the season. The dining area is located under the volume of the upper floor where the master bedroom is located.

The concrete panels used on the exterior have a 30% content of natural fibers. In the yard, a teak platform completely surrounded by volcanic stones gives warmth to the space.

Materials such as wood were used in combination with concrete panels on the façade. The large glassed surfaces are mainly used to allow natural light to enter the house unhindered, and also to optimize cross ventilation.

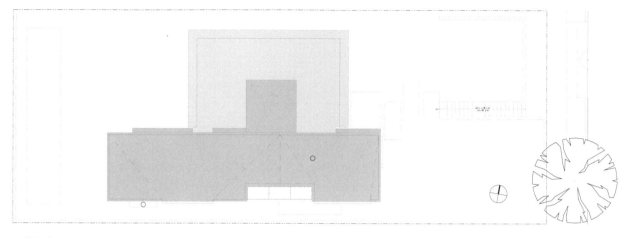

Site plan

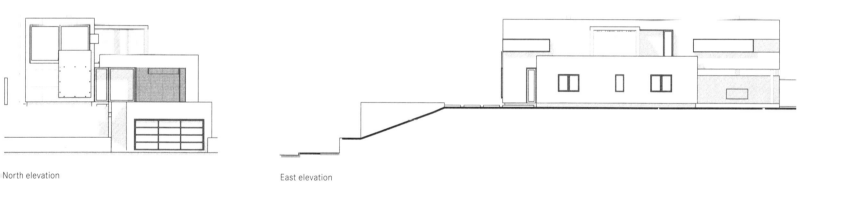

North elevation

East elevation

South elevation

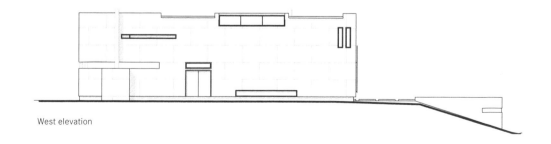

West elevation

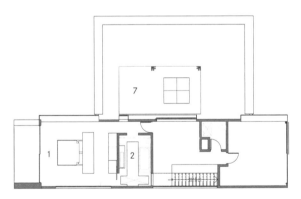

1. Bedroom
2. Bathroom
3. Kitchen
4. Dining room
5. Living area
6. Lounge
7. Terrace

Upper level

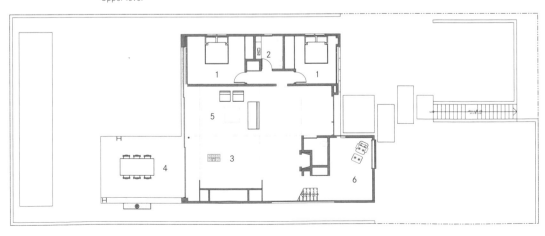

Lower level

The kitchen furniture is lined in tire rubber. This space-saving furniture includes chairs that store away. The orange Corian countertop is reminiscent of lava from Icelandic volcanoes.

The lower floor is laid out as an open space to enhance ventilation and natural light. Skylights above the staircase allow sunlight to enter and make energy saving possible.

Klein Bottle House

Rob McBride & Debbie-Lyn Ryan

Location **Mornington Peninsula, Australia**
Surface area **2,780 sq ft**
Construction **2007**
© **John Gollings**

Thermal inertia, cross ventilation

Rainwater collection

Certified sustainable wood

Sloping terrain

Temperate wet without a dry season

Architects McBride and Ryan designed Klein Bottle House influenced by two concepts: the Moebius strip, where a continuous, unending surface is warped by passing from the interior to the exterior; and origami, where the final form is understood as the result of multiple folds.

CAD technology played an important part in the entire design process. It made the development of complex surfaces possible from mathematical functions, and allowed these surfaces to be built by means of breaking up the structure and the walls. The architects described the design in the following way: "While the building follows tradition as far as functionality goes, it experiments with geometric variation in the creation of new forms and ends up satisfying the client's needs and desires."

The house is located on the Mornington Peninsula, one and a half hours from Melbourne. The dwelling is completely isolated, submerged in an area of dense bush land on sand dunes and very near the empty beaches of the location. The cantilevered extension of the shell and the presence of trees lessen the sun's action, while the trees create flowing visual movement that can be appreciated from inside the house.

The plan of the house revolves around a central courtyard and a staircase that, as it rises, connects it to the different spaces located on different levels. The courtyard receives natural light and cross ventilation provided by the sea breeze. Rainwater is stored in storage tanks located under the children's room. The bedroom and living area open onto a deck made of wood sourced from sustainable forestry. Both spaces open out fully to the forest and the natural setting.

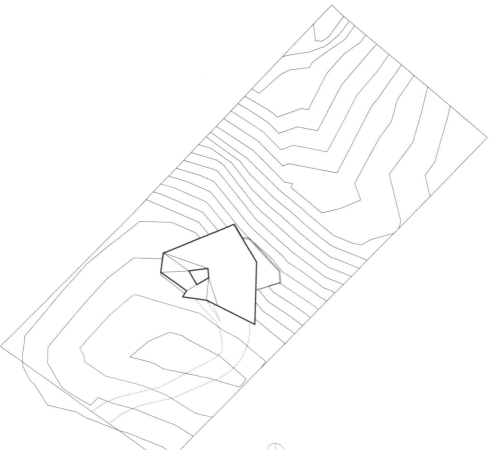

Site plan

To reach the dwelling, it is necessary to take a winding track between the forest and the sand dunes. From there the house can be seen in the midst of the vegetation. The shell is made of fibrous cement panels and sheet metal painted black.

The living area, kitchen, and dining room share the same surface and open to the landscape through sliding glass doors. The interior is extended out to two wooden decks, one facing east and the other north. The living room floor is bamboo from a sustainable plantation and is finished in natural varnish.

View from the stairs and the central courtyard. Three types of flooring were used exclusively throughout the house: carpet, natural stone, and wood.

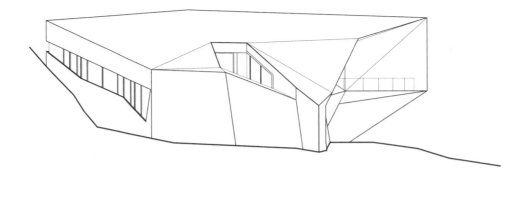

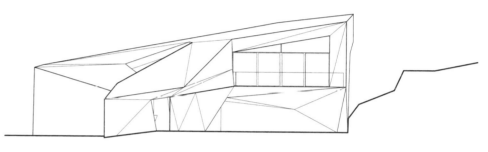

Elevations

The main bathroom is faced in natural black stone and the floor is glass mosaic tiles. The vanity top is a synthetic resin and quartz agglomerate.

The color scheme of the interior revolves around the combination of three colors: red defines activities; through the shell, black establishes a dialogue between interior and exterior; and finally, white unifies the entire surface of the house.

Elevations
As if they were paper figures, the four walls take on different forms and create different spatial volumes, each with their particular characteristics that differentiate them from the others.

Floor plan
The form achieved is based on the concept of origami. Emphasis is given to the master bedroom and living area; both face east and are in visual contact with the beach.

Floor plan

1. Foyer
2. Courtyard
3. Laundry
4. Kids' room
5. Bedroom
6. Living/dining
7. East deck
8. North deck

The Wave House

Tony Owen NDM

Location **Bondi Beach, Sydney, Australia**
Surface area **2,210 sq ft**
Construction **2007**
© **Brett Boardman**

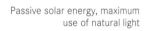

Passive solar energy, maximum
use of natural light

Faucets with water-saving systems

Locally sourced materials,
UV protection glass

Flat terrain

Subtropical oceanic, yearly average
of 180 days of rain

This house is located on Bondi Beach, only 4.4 miles from the central business district of Sydney, world-renowned for its surfing competitions. The climate of the region has warm summers and mild winters, with temperatures that vary between a maximum of 27 °C and a minimum of 5 °C. Energy saving and passive climate control were two priority elements of the design of this residence.

The house clearly responds to its location and offers a dual design: beach house and urban dwelling. The living area resembles a local café, while the roof curves reflect the waves on the beach. This relationship between exterior and interior is a unifying element seen throughout the house: the curves of the roof begin at the entrance to the garage and grow in height over the living room, at the north end.

The lower level was built using concrete blocks, while the upper floor is clad in frosted glass to allow light to enter. This transition is reinforced by the excellent use of various materials that represent different layers or strata.

The design of lighting plays a major role. On the upper level, the windows open to the exterior, enabling natural light to enter throughout the day. On the lower floor, incoming light is more diffused as metal membranes act as solar protection and prevent the interior space from becoming too hot.

There are also touches of luxury in the interior: the master bedroom has a bar, and there is a free-standing bath in an open en-suite.

North elevation

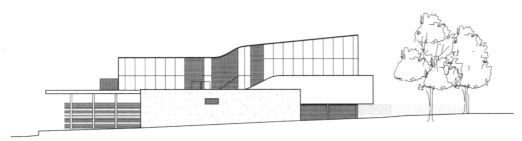

East elevation

South elevation

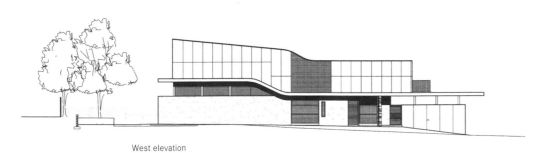

West elevation

The interrelation between exterior and interior is maximized throughout the house. The large projected structures provide shade to the spaces behind the façade.

The concrete floor slabs act as necessary thermal mass for winter nights. As changes in temperature are gentle in this climate, the use of this type of feature is sufficient to maintain interior comfort.

North elevation
The north façade makes extensive use of glass to favor natural light.

East and west elevations
The play on wave shapes can be observed on the east and west façades.

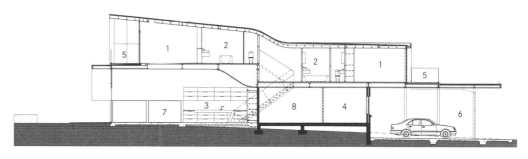

North-south section

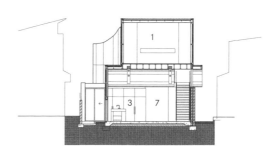

East-west section

1. Bedroom
2. Bathroom
3. Kitchen
4. Study
5. Terrace
6. Garage
7. Dining room
8. Game room

The transition between exterior and interior is gradual. The use of the same floor covering in the living area and on the terrace creates an effect of continuity.

The ceiling curves and certain details in furnishings — for example, the kitchen table — are reminiscent of waves on the sea.

The bath in the master bedroom is situated in an open space with views to the exterior.

The simple and minimal use of materials permit curves and lines to interrelate.

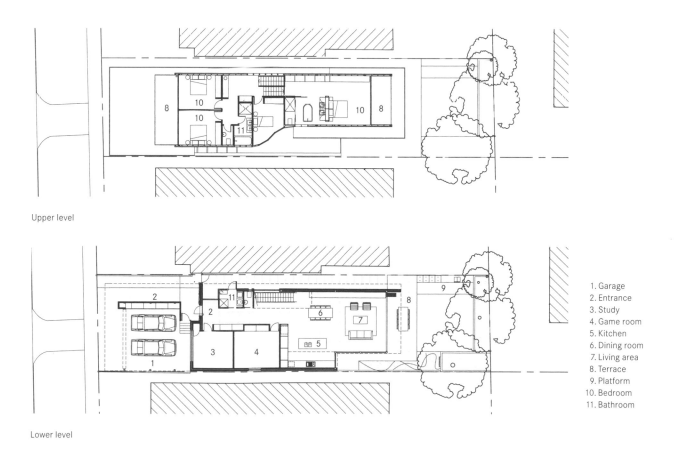

Upper level

Lower level

1. Garage
2. Entrance
3. Study
4. Game room
5. Kitchen
6. Dining room
7. Living area
8. Terrace
9. Platform
10. Bedroom
11. Bathroom

Johanna House

Nicholas Burns Associates

Location **Johanna, Victoria, Australia**
Surface area **1,880 sq ft**
Construction **2006**
© **Earl Carter**

Passive solar energy, cross ventilation

Rainwater collection, wastewater treatment

Rammed earth

Slightly sloping terrain

Semi-arid with average annual rainfall of between 7.9 and 15.8 inch

This house is located in Johanna, a small beach town in Victoria famous for the surf competitions held in the vicinity. It was designed by Nicholas Burns Associates, an architectural studio that has been guided since its founding with the philosophy of environmentally friendly construction. This dwelling has four bedrooms, two bathrooms and an open space for the kitchen, dining room, and living area.

This residence is on 40 hectares of pristine bush land adjoining a national park with extensive views of the ocean, and is particularly well-known for its flora and fauna. Owing to the great importance of the vegetation in this setting, no trees were cut during the construction of the house. Materials used were rammed earth, concrete, glass, and steel in small quantities, in order to achieve the discreet insertion of the house into the landscape. Glass walls around most of the perimeter open the house up to the landscape and create a dialogue with nature.

The glass on the façade features ultraviolet protection to comply with energy efficiency requirements. As the temperature rarely dips below 13 °C in this area, the heat stored in the walls and floors is enough to maintain a comfortable temperature in the house at night. During summer, the interior is cooled by cross ventilation, achieved through the strategic placement of windows.

Rainwater is captured and stored in tanks. It is used in sanitary fixtures and for fire protection, and also as drinking water after filtering. Wastewater is treated on site biologically by means of a sand filter 4.9 ft deep without the use of chemicals.

The glass façade opens to the best views of the sea. The expansive projecting roof offers shade and protects the rooms from the strong sun. The floor-to ceiling windows on both sides allow air currents to form which ventilate the rooms naturally.

The rammed earth walls on the sides of the dwelling act as thermal storage. They were built with a thickness of 11.8 inch and protect the private areas of the house. Morning light allows the rustic texture of the rammed earth to be appreciated. This was made with compacting techniques of blocks comprising four layers.

Exterior paving makes use of local gravel, a material that suits the design perfectly.

Site plan
The house is adapted to the terrain, and the access road was especially built for it.

Elevations
The west elevation has the largest expanse of glass; the other three are protected from solar radiation by rammed earth walls.

Site plan

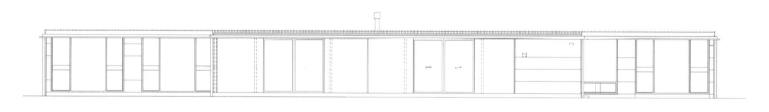

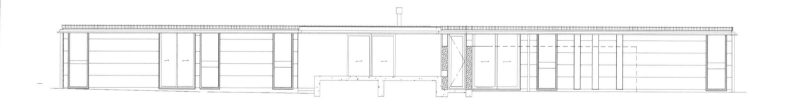

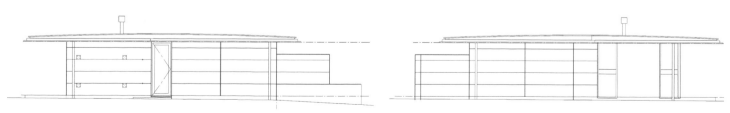

Elevations

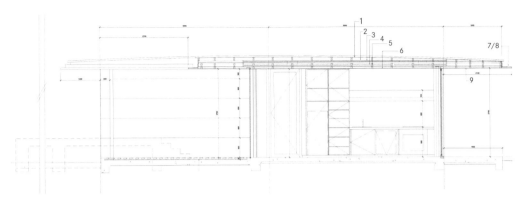

A-A section

1. Stramit Bushland Grey studs
2. 2 x R2.5 insulation on both sides
3. Wooden battens 35.4 x 17.7 inch for every 472 inch
4. 5.9 x 2.7-inch structural steel
5. Wooden beams 4.1 / 7.8 x 1.8 inch for every 236 inch
6. 0.5-inch drywall
7. 0.08-inch thick aluminum border
8. Powder coat to match
9. 0.6-inch thick fibrous cement panel

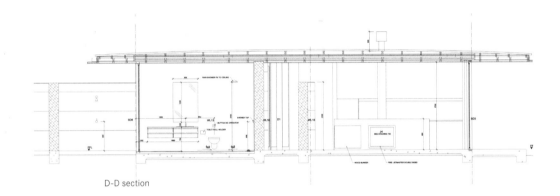

D-D section

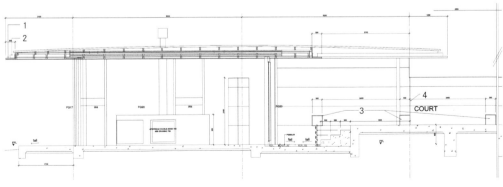

E-E section

1. 0.08-inch thick aluminum border
2. 5.9 x 3.9-inch channel
3. 11.8 x 11.8-inch holes in rammed earth wall
4. Joint

Rammed earth is commonly used building material in Australia. It is based on a combination of craft techniques and new technology to achieve greater durability. The bedrooms and bathrooms have rammed earth walls, and the tiles are placed over a lattice frame made of steel and wood members.

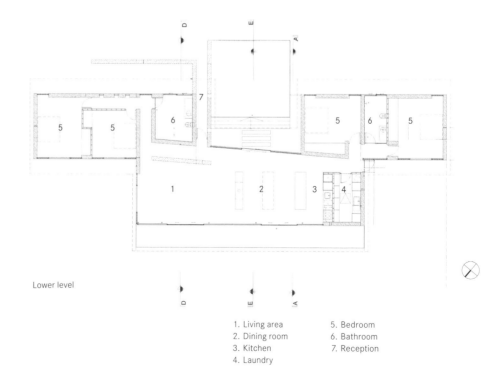

Lower level

1. Living area
2. Dining room
3. Kitchen
4. Laundry
5. Bedroom
6. Bathroom
7. Reception

A central fireplace heats the rooms on winter nights. The double box that give it shape is laser-cut steel with a thickness of 0.4 inch. The hearth is surrounded by a double layer of stone to increase thermal mass.

Panel House

David Randall Hertz/SEA – Studio of Environmental
Architecture

Location **Venice Beach, CA, USA**
Surface area **2,910 sq ft**
Construction **2004**
© **Juergen Nogai**

Photovoltaic and thermal solar energy

Renewable, recyclable, and non-toxic
materials

Flat terrain

Temperate Mediterranean and dry all year
around

From the start, there were two issues to resolve regarding the design of the house: taking advantage of the sea views, with the problem of intense solar radiation posed by a west-facing orientation; and the need to safeguard the privacy of the occupants of the house located on the popular Ocean Front Walk by the beach in Los Angeles, California.

These conditions, and the constraints of a narrow plot, meant that the project began with a series of angled walls and side patios to provide views from the hallways and different areas of the house. The space created between the walls is used for the placement of pivoted windows that allow breezes to be controlled. Ventilation comes from the sea, crosses the house and exits via the down-wind part of the building.

Conditioned by the narrowness of the site, the frame was designed using large-section steel columns and beams, combined with diagonal struts. The floor consisted of a grid made from steel frames and small concrete slabs. This design enabled load-bearing walls to be dispensed with and gave greater freedom in the layout of internal partition walls.

The house is clad in panels of thick synthetic foam panels with an enameled aluminum skin on both internal and external surfaces. Each panel can be fitted by just two people, and they are installed by screwing them to closure plates on the edges of the floor slabs of each of the levels of the house. This walling system reduces construction time and does not generate waste.

In addition to natural ventilation, the house is equipped with a complete system of solar protection including louvers and tinted glass that do not block the views. Part of the power supply comes from the installation of 14 photovoltaic panels generating an average of 2.3 kW per day. The hot water system and radiant floor heating receive a large proportion of their energy from the thermal solar panels on the roof.

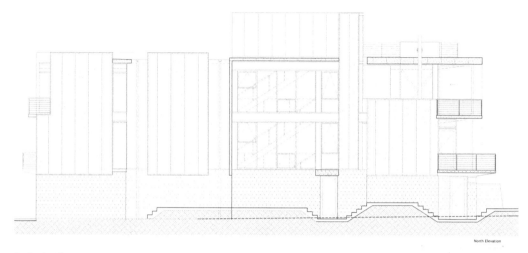

North elevation

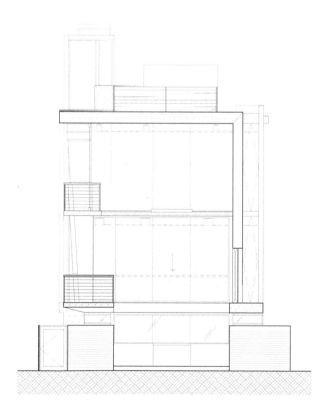

West elevation

Section of entrance wall and
window with motor-operated
automatic vertical movement
system.

The prefabricated panels are covered with sheet aluminum. This
surface reflects the changing colors of the sky and sunsets.

179

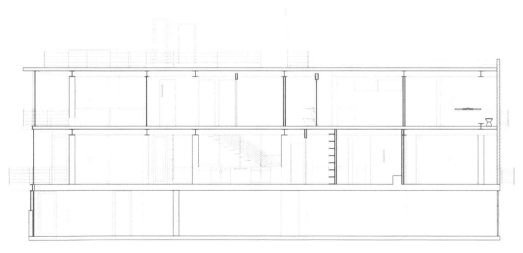

West-east section

In addition to the stairs, the house has a hydraulic glass elevator giving easy access to the roof, where there are photovoltaic and thermal solar panels.

The metal and wood frame of the staircase act as a solar chimney. Hot air leaves through the skylights in summer.

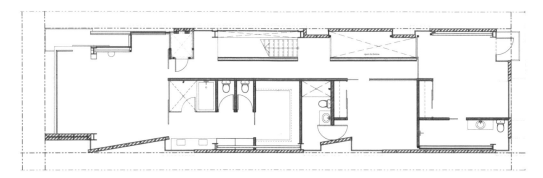

Upper level

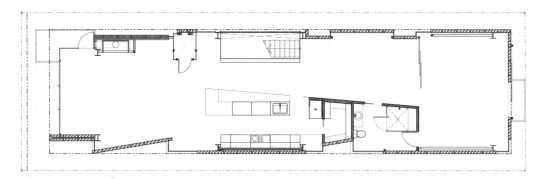

Middle level

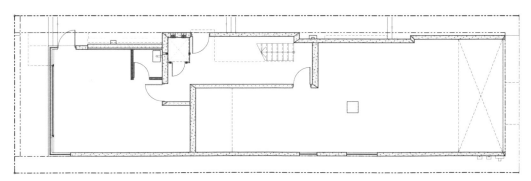

Lower level

The requirements for thermal insulation are important in dwellings in order to avoid heat loss or to generate heat gain and therefore save on energy use. In this case, louvers were designed to provide shade for windows, which reduces solar radiation inside.

Cabinets and countertops in both the kitchen and bathroom are of stainless steel and FSC-certified walnut. Polished concrete was used for all floor surfaces.

Upper level / middle level / lower level
This house is located on site bordering other buildings. The project has a basically vertical design; the connecting elements are the staircase and elevator. The lower level has a side entrance and an area for guests. The middle level contains the kitchen, dining room, and living area. The upper level has bedrooms and bathrooms. Interesting views can be seen from the front of the house.

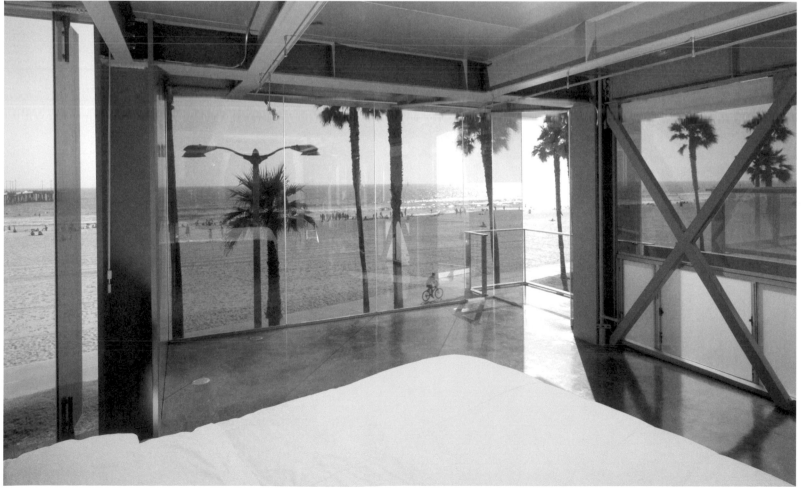

Taroona 2

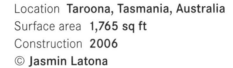

Room 11 Studio PTY LTD

Location **Taroona, Tasmania, Australia**
Surface area **1,765 sq ft**
Construction **2006**
© **Jasmin Latona**

Radiant floor heating

Faucets with water-saving systems

Natural, renewable and recyclable materials

Sloping terrain

Slightly humid temperate maritime

The site of Taroona 2 has a steep slope, so the dwelling has been laid out over four stepped levels. A series of terraces and stairs link the interior with the exterior. Access is through the uppermost level, from where one descends until a bridge is reached connecting with the next level. Stairs lead down through the levels to the structure on the lowest level, containing a studio. This stepped design allows all of the spaces to enjoy views of the Derwent River and mountainous landscape.

Manufactured materials — glass panes and steel profiles — and those of natural and local origin — wooden flooring and gravel on outdoor ground areas — are united with a construction system mainly involving dry assembly. At the end of the useful life of the building, the materials can be recovered by dismantling instead of the traditional demolition.

The frame consists of a grid of steel pillars over reinforced concrete plinths and held in place by a series of perimeter beams. By laying foundations at specific points only, most of the roots of the numerous trees on the site were saved. The skin of the structure is made of wooden posts and uprights clad on the outside with plywood panels that afford insulation and rigidity at the same time.

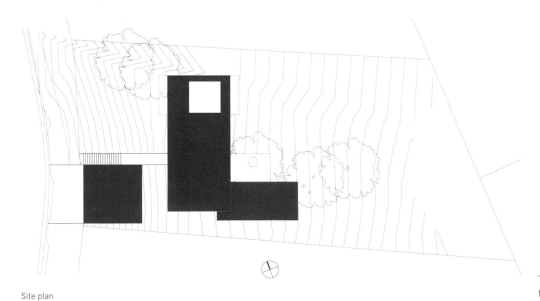

Site plan

The layout of the decks lengthways in relation to the slope of the terrain offers views over the distant river. The other direction, perpendicular to the slope, offers predominant views of the vegetation.

External facings are of natural and industrial materials: the former includes gravel and wood decking, and the latter includes extruded and galvanized steel, plywood panels, and extruded aluminum frames.

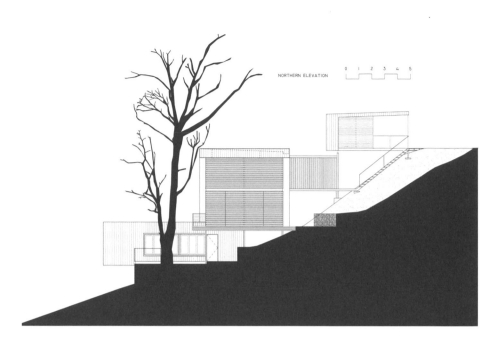

NORTHERN ELEVATION   0 1 2 3 4 5

Longitudinal elevation

Longitudinal section

Longitudinal elevation
Plywood panels and locally sourced oak louvers dominate the
north façade, together with glass. The upper level contains the
entrance to the house, and the lower level is a study.

Longitudinal section
The independent frame of the steel pillars, the reinforced
concrete foundations, and the stepped design of the volumes
adapted to the slope allow the project to be inserted into the
landscape.

The interior spaces are open plan: they were designed to favor visual connection.

Different hues of wood used on interior and exterior floors, and in the fittings of the open kitchen, are combined with white plasterboard panels on walls and ceilings.

The interior space was designed as a prism with strong connection with the exterior through large windows and decks. The complete effect of space can be seen from the lower level, owing to the lack of visual barriers and the upper floor being withdrawn to give continuity to the façade, which is treated like a curtain wall.

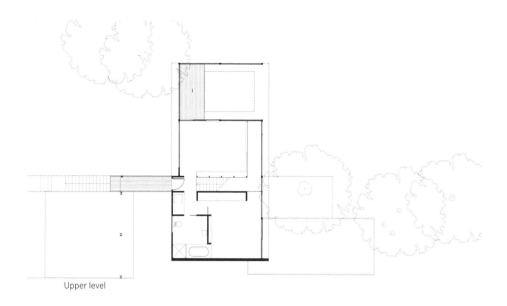

Upper level

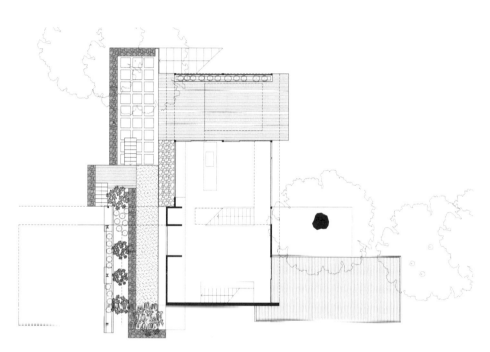

Middle level

Upper level
The third level up from the bottom houses the bedroom, a second study and a deck-like balcony with river views.

Middle level
The second level up is an open-plan space that is open to the exterior through large floor-to-ceiling windows. The decks offer views of the river, mountains, and vegetation.

Lower level
The lowest level contains the study. A great effort was made to preserve the vegetation. The frame and foundations were made without cutting down any trees.

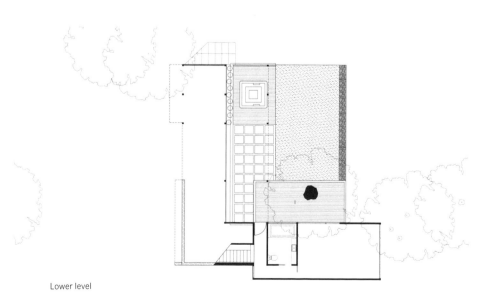

Lower level

Sustainable Architecture Glossary

Air conditioning systems: the simultaneous control of temperature, humidity, and movement and quality of air inside a space.

Boiler: combination of generator and burner designed to transmit heat from combustion to water.

Climate zones: zones defined according to the severity of climatic conditions in winter (A, B, C, D, E) and summer (1, 2, 3, 4).

Effective energy demand: energy required to maintain the interior of a building in legally defined conditions of comfort depending on the use of the building and the climate zone where it is located. It covers the energy demand for climate control (HVAC) systems, corresponding to months of the heating or cooling season.

Energy performance certificate for buildings: recognized certificate, including the energy efficiency rating for a building calculated according to a scale developed for this purpose.

Heat/cooling load: amount of energy required in an area in order to maintain certain conditions of temperature and humidity for a specific application; for example, thermal comfort.

Humidity: amount of water vapor present in the air. It can be expressed in absolute or relative terms.

Luminous efficacy: the ratio of the luminous flux emitted by a light source to power consumed by the source.

Photovoltaic solar panel: device using solar radiation energy to generate electricity.

Solar factor: ratio of the total energy passing through glass to the incident solar energy.

Solar radiation: energy coming from the sun in the form of electromagnetic waves.

Thermal comfort: satisfaction of a person with a specific thermal environment.

Thermal habitability: conditions of temperature, humidity, and air speed of an environment producing an adequate and sufficient sensation of well-being for the people in that environment.

Thermal inertia: capacity of a material to store received thermal energy and release it progressively; in this way the need for HVAC systems is lessened.

Thermal insulation: capacity of materials to resist the passing of heat through conduction. All materials offer resistance, to a greater or lesser degree, to heat passing through them.

Thermal mass: capacity of a material to retain heat.

Thermal solar panel: device designed to absorb solar radiation and transfer the energy produced to a working flow circulating inside it.

Bibliography

Costa Duran, Sergi. *Green Homes: New Ideas for Sustainable Living*. New York: Collins Design, 2007.

Fairs, Marcus. *Green Design*. London: Carlton Publishing, 2008.

Gauzin-Muller, Dominique. *25 casas ecológicas*. Barcelona: Editorial Gustavo Gili, 2006.

Baraona Pohl, Ethel; Reyes, César; and Pirillo, Claudio. *Arquitectura sostenible*. Alboraya: Editorial Pencil, 2007.

Roaf, Sue. *Ecohouse*. Kidlington: Elsevier, 2007.

Schleifer, Simone. *Pequeñas casas ecológicas*. Cologne: Evergreen – Taschen, 2007.

Solanas, Toni. *Vivienda y sostenibilidad en España Vol. 1*. Barcelona: Editorial Gustavo Gili, 2007

Directory

Arquitectura X
Av. Granda Centeno 1114 y Bobadilla 16
Quito, Ecuador
T: +593 9 4502573
amoreno@arquitecturax.com
www.arquitecturax.com

Beals Arquitectos
Chile
T: +56 2 881 8485
alejandrobeals@gmail.com

Belzberg Architects
1501 Colorado Ave., Suite B
Santa Monica, CA 90404, USA
T: +1 310 453 9611
info@belzbergarchitects.com
www.belzbergarchitects.com

Correia/Ragazzi Arquitectos
Rua Azevedo Coutinho 39, 4º andar, sala 44
4100-100 Porto, Portugal
T: +351 226 067 047
correiaragazzi@gmail.com
www.correiaragazzi.com

David Patricio Barragán Andrade
Las Casas OE3-244 y Av. América
Quito, Ecuador
david00b@gmail.com
www.albordearq.com

David Randall Hertz/SEA
Studio of Environmental Architecture
1920 Olympic Blvd.
Santa Monica, CA 90404, USA
T: +1 310 829 9932
inquiries@studioea.com
www.studioea.com

Durbach Block Architects
Level 5, 71 York Street
Sydney NSW 2000, Australia
T: +61 2 8297 3500
mail@durbachblock.com
www.durbachblock.com

Felipe Assadi & Francisca Pulido
CP 7550056
Santiago de Chile, Chile
T: +56 2 234 5558
info@assadi.cl
www.assadi.cl

G Ateliers
203 Columbia Street
Brooklyn, NY 11231, USA
T: +1 718 260 9620
info@gateliers.com
www.gateliers.com

Giovanni D'Ambrosio
Via Monserrato 34
00187 Rome, Italy
T: +39 06 686 9760
vanbergen_dambrosio@hotmail.com
www.giovannidambrosio.com

Jackson Clements Burrows Architects
One Harwood Place
Melbourne VIC 3000, Australia
T: +61 3 9654 6227
jacksonclementsburrows@jcba.com.au
www.jcba.com.au

José María Sáez Vaquero
Galápagos OE3-196 y Vargas
Quito, Ecuador
T: +593 2 2955434
2josemoni@gmail.com
www.arqsaez.com

McBride Charles Ryan
4/21 Wynnstay Road
Prahran VIC 3101, Australia
T: +61 3 9510 1006
mail@mcbridecharlesryan.com.au
www.mcbridecharlesryan.com.au

Minarc Architects
2324 Michigan Ave.
Santa Monica, CA 90404, USA
T: +1 310 998 8899
james@minarc.com
www.minarc.com

Nicholas Burns Associates
Singapore
T: +65 6738 0064
nb@nicholas-burns.com
www.nicholas-burns.com

Ofis Arhitekti
Kongresni Trg 3
1000 Ljubljana, Slovenia
T: +386 1 426 0085
projekt@ofis-a.si
www.ofis-a.si

Pugh & Scarpa
2525 Michigan Ave., F1
Santa Monica, CA 90404, USA
T: +1 310 828 0226
info@pugh-scarpa.com
www.pugh-scarpa.com

Ray Kappe
715 Brooktree Road
Pacific Palisades, CA 90272, USA
T: +1 310 459 7791
info@kappedu.com
www.kappedu.com
www.livinghomes.net

Room 11 Studio PTY LTD
Level 2, Room 11, 64-68 Liverpool Street
Bank Arcade 7000 TAS, Australia
T: +61 3 6234 2847
info@room11.com.au
www.room11.com.au

SSD – Architecture + Urbanism
215w 40th Street, 7R
New York, NY 10018, USA
T: +1 212 248 7500
info@ssdarchitecture.com
www.ssdarchitecture.com

Studios Architecture
99 Green Street
San Francisco, CA 94111, USA
T: +1 415 398 7575
la-info@studiosarch.com
www.studiosarch.com

Tony Owen NDM
260 Young Street
Annandale NSW 2038, Australia
T: +61 2 9571 1700
info@tondm.com.au
www.tonyowen.com.au

Tuomo Siitonen Architects
Veneentekijäntie 12
00210 Helsinki, Finland
T: +358 9 8569 5533
info@tsi.fi
www.tsi.fi

Una Arquitetos
Rua General Jardim 770, 13A
Vila Buarque, São Paulo, Brazil
T: +55 11 3231 3080
una@unaarquitetos.com.br
www.unaarquitetos.com.br

Víctor Cañas, Andrés Cañas
San Pedro Montes de Oca
Apartado 340-2050, Costa Rica
T: +506 2253 2112
victor@canas.co.cr
www.victor.canas.co.cr

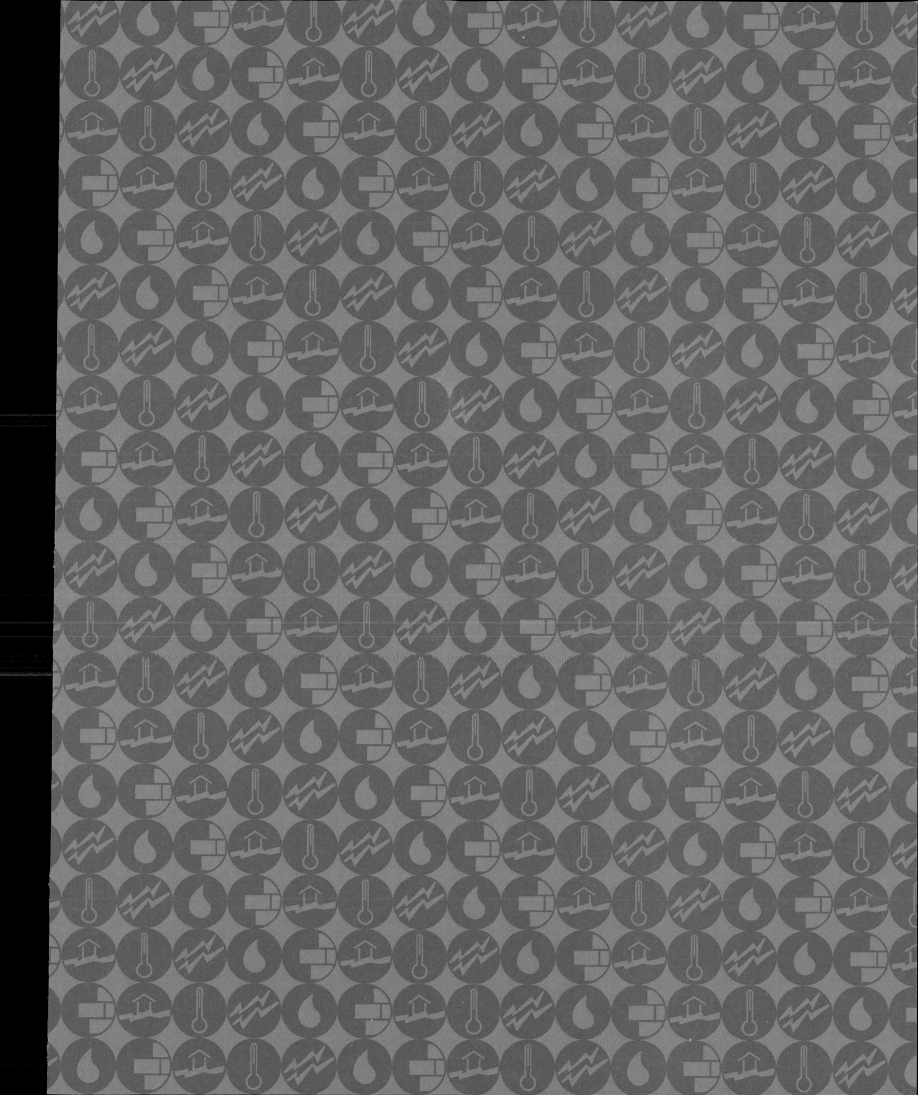